PAINTINGS OF CATASTROPHIC

ENVIRONMENTAL CHANGE

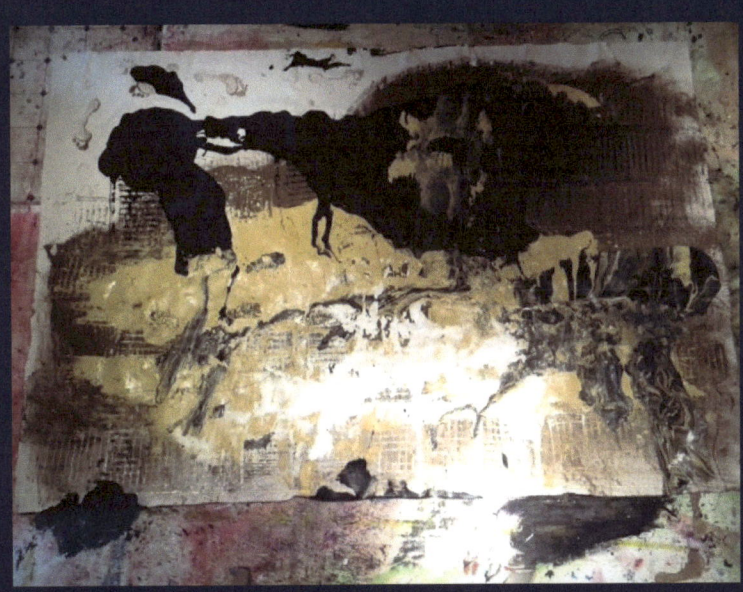

GARY WALTERS

VECTOR PRINT AND PUBLISHING

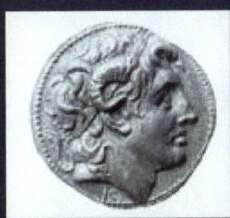

The world heats up

Glaciers melt at the poles

A tsunami reaches a coastal city

Pollution sifts through the atmosphere

Oil spills into a city

Rivers run red with blood and toxins

The Great Pacific Garbage Patch

The Cascadia Subduction zone ruptures

Each of the paintings in this series is about the current environment on Planet Earth. They are large and messy and were done with house paint and brooms and squeegees and hands and feet. They were done on the floor of my studio. They were done in a state of near rage for it is hard to push painting itself into the dire straits and huge movements that we are now witnessing. And also you fight the feeling that it doesn't make any difference.

Nevertheless I present them. Each painting is followed by details from that work which I think show the vastly interconnected nature of whatever happens here. The microcosmic and the macrocosmic scales and the organic basis of our lives are clearly seen. There are two cities, each imperiled.

We know that the increase in population on earth combined with global warming whether a natural cycle or manmade or both are going to cause immense disruption. A warming earth melts the ice at the poles causing the oceans to rise. Weather patterns alter causing drought where there was none and floods where it had been dry. The tidal flows from large storms endanger coastlines as well.

Heat in the atmosphere is captured and remains. The constant outflows of pollutants from every sort of manufacture is also caught there and remains and then descends to further poison the earth.

We know that the various anti-biotics used to counter infection are losing their race with the mutability of germs. We are told there might soon be nothing left to stop the spread of infection. We are also becoming immune to some of them because so many are used to grow the food we eat. Interventions in the natural cycles of plants and animals looks like short term gain. These same medications and everything you could think of often ends up in rivers in a recombinant mess that is highly toxic.

We all know that the plastic that wraps everything so that it can be moved and sold and preserved as well as objects of all kinds designed to be disposable but not biodegradable are rapidly creating a vast gyre of garbage as it eventually reaches the seas and flowing with the currents gathers together. The size of the accumulations is enormous. I show one such gyre. It was the dirtiest and messiest of all the paintings to do. I used oil based and acrylic paint which don't mix, don't blend.

I show an oil spill on the outskirts of a city where oil is collected and refined. There is as yet no fire.

The Juan de Fuca plate and the North American Plate for example are part of the constant shift of tectonic forces pushing against each other. Eventually something must give. The above mentioned plates are near such a moment. This will cause an earthquake and tsunami all along the North American Pacific coast. It is estimated that it is more dangerous than the San Andreas Fault further south. And calculations have shown quite recently that this spring back is just about due. I show the earthquake that would follow the release of centuries of pressure on these tectonic plates.

There is the challenge of showing these subjects in a painting, however unpleasant, ugly, and frightening. What everyone is doing to help the environment is an ever more conscious series of activities, yet the scale of a Nature aroused combined with what we are not doing presents an apocalyptic picture.

There is no argument here. The facts are plain and available. It seems incredible that building still takes place in vulnerable low lying coastal areas such as

Florida or the south Atlantic seaboard of the United States. It seems incredible that the wealth of companies and nations is not directed at planning for eventual catastrophe. It seems incredible that wars continue with more and more refugees living lives of the utmost suffering and providing the very ground for the outbreak of a pestilence.

There is no argument here because all this is well known. So my paintings are more of a testament to this critical period in our history. A showing. A reminding. A telling. And a release of the tectonic pressures within my own being faced as we all are with the potential for catastrophic extinctions.

Gary Walters

2015

The world heats up

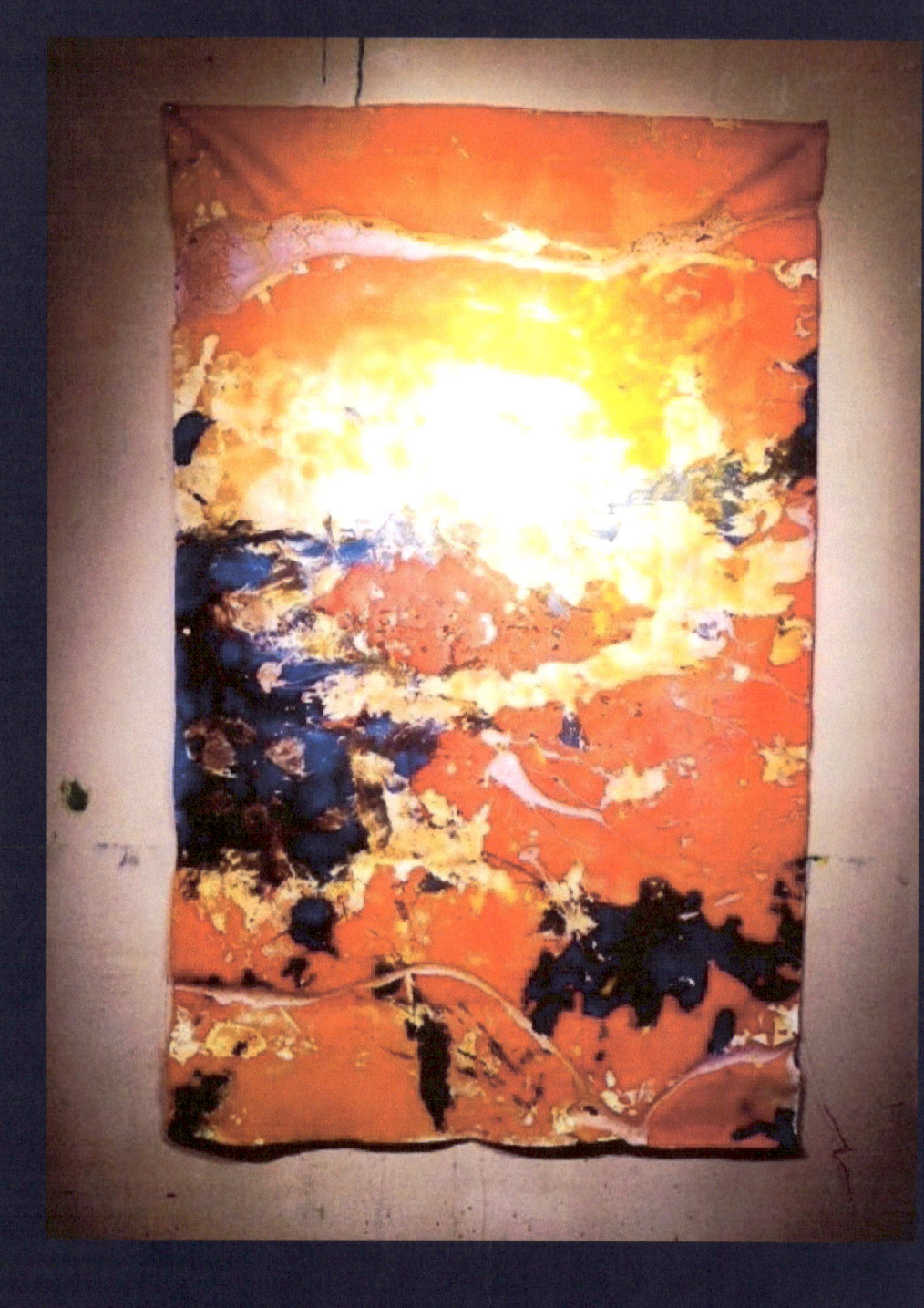

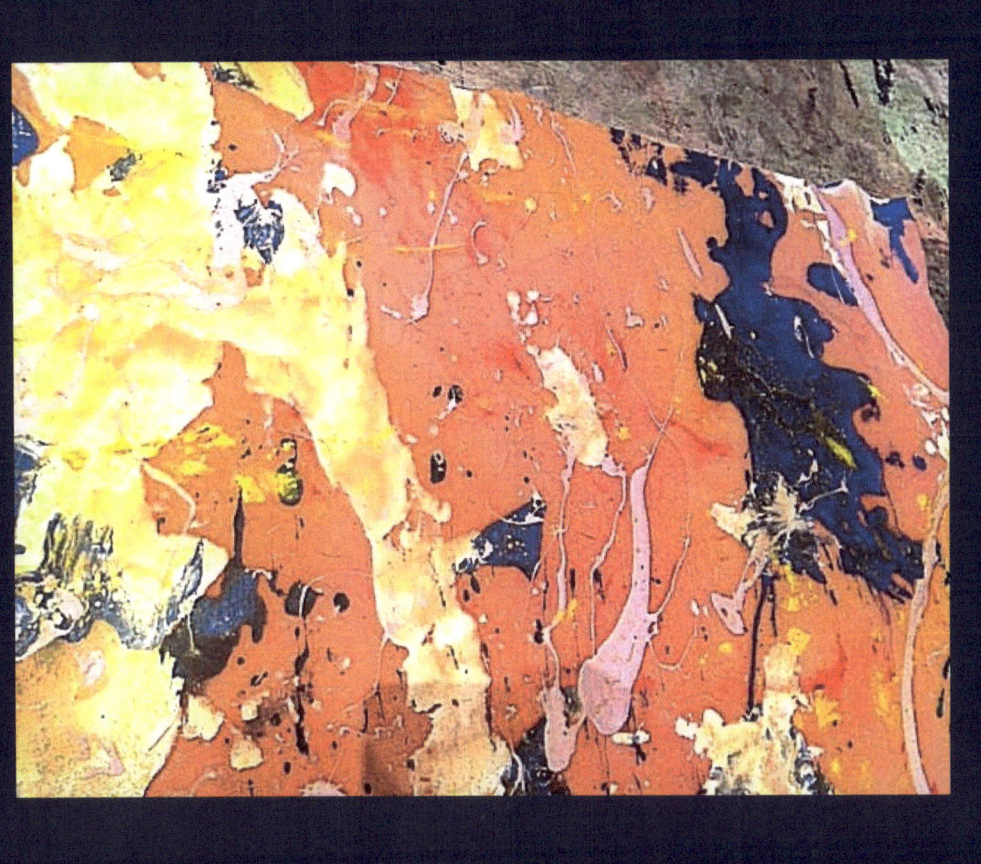

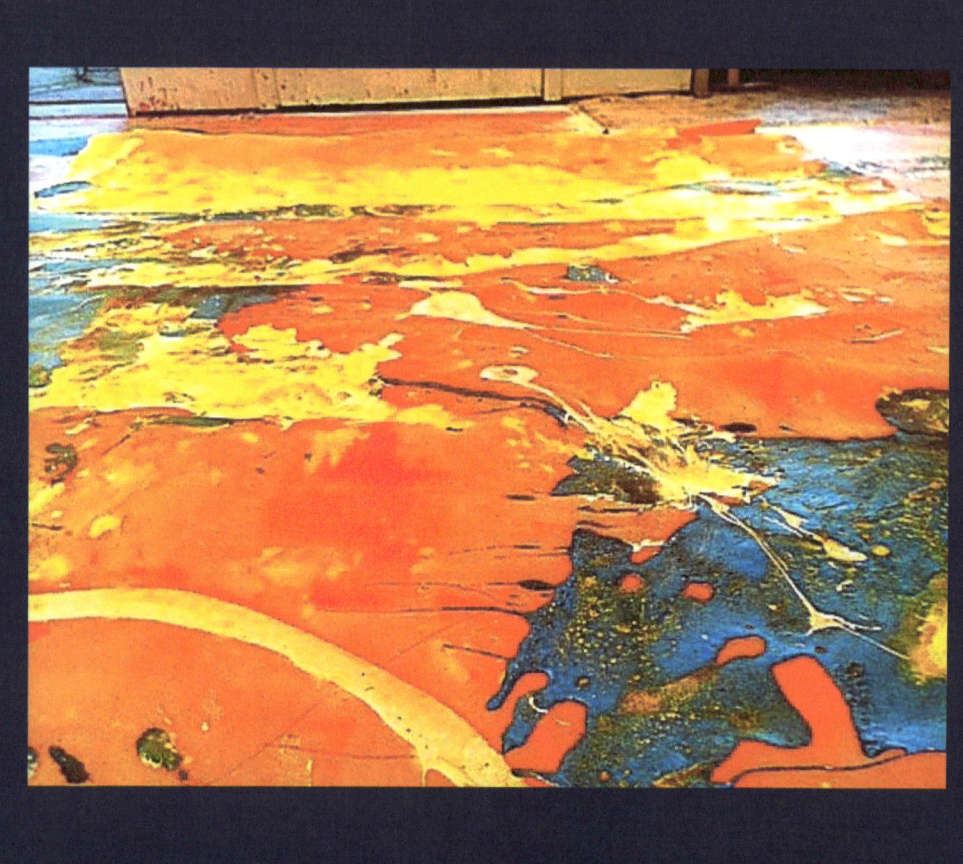

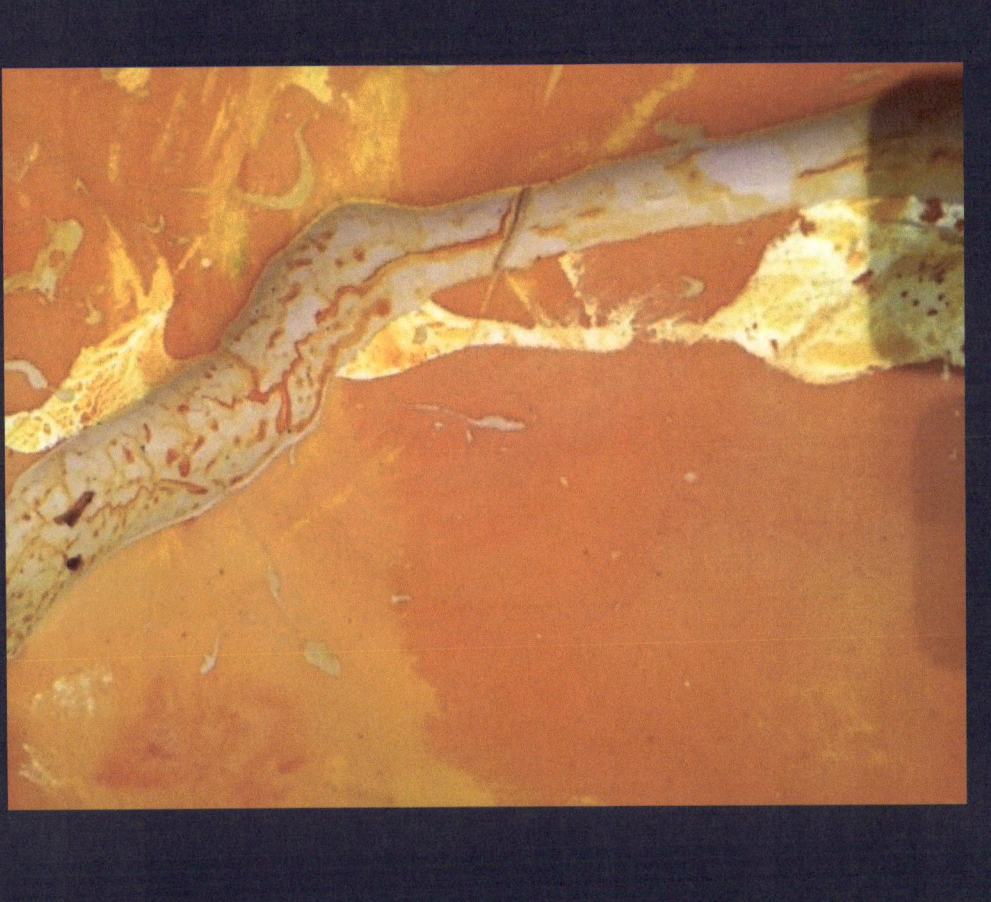

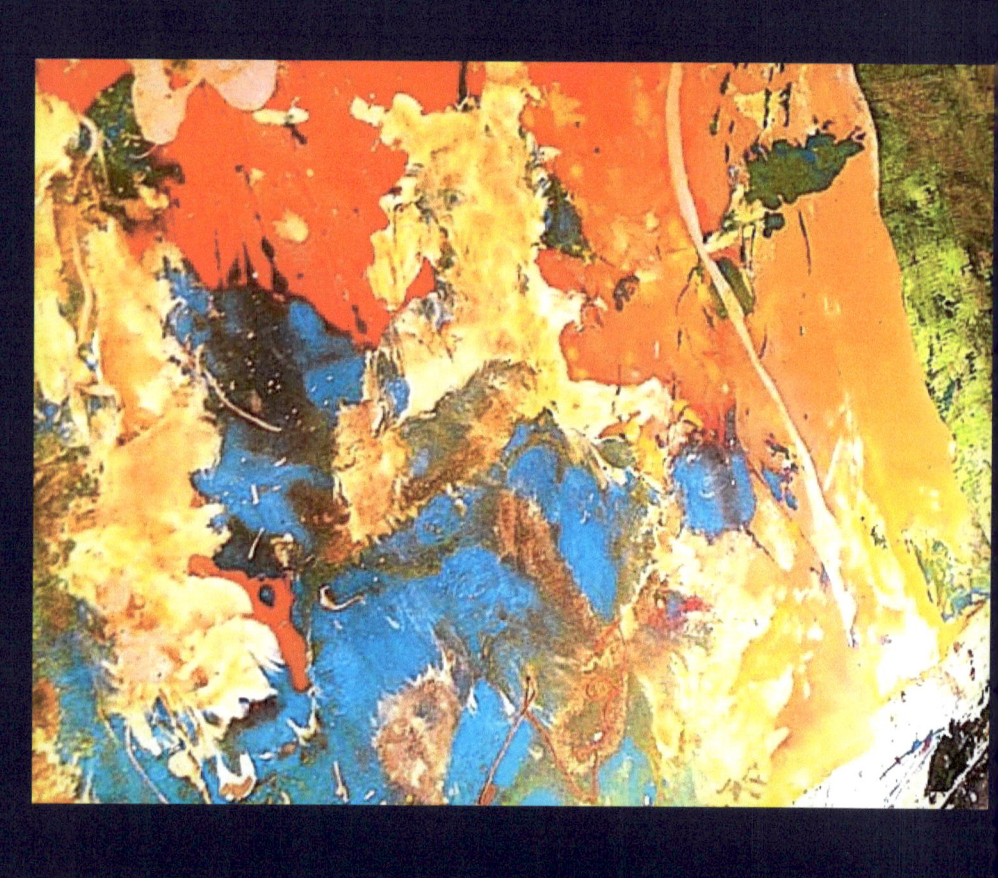

Glaciers melt at the poles

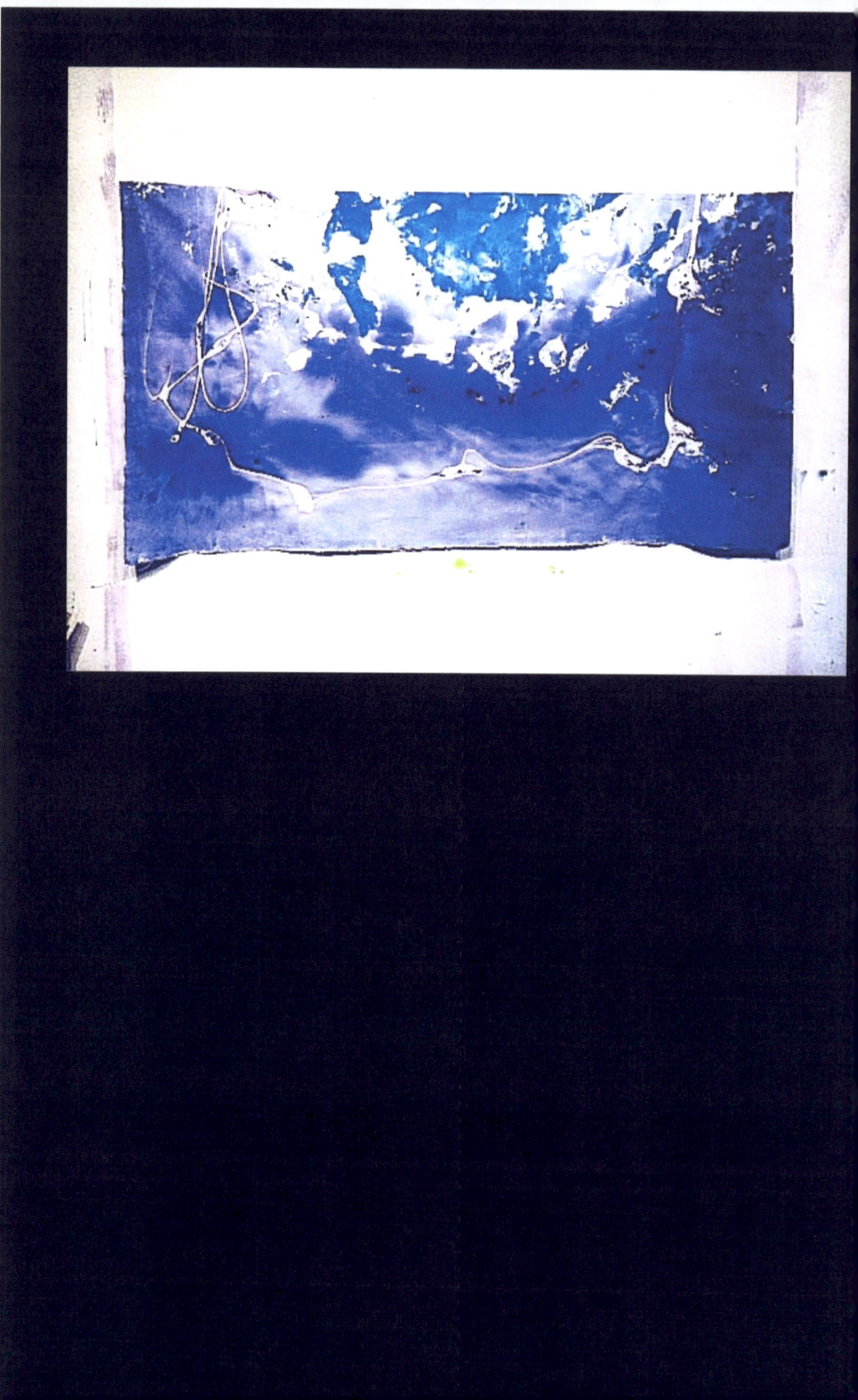

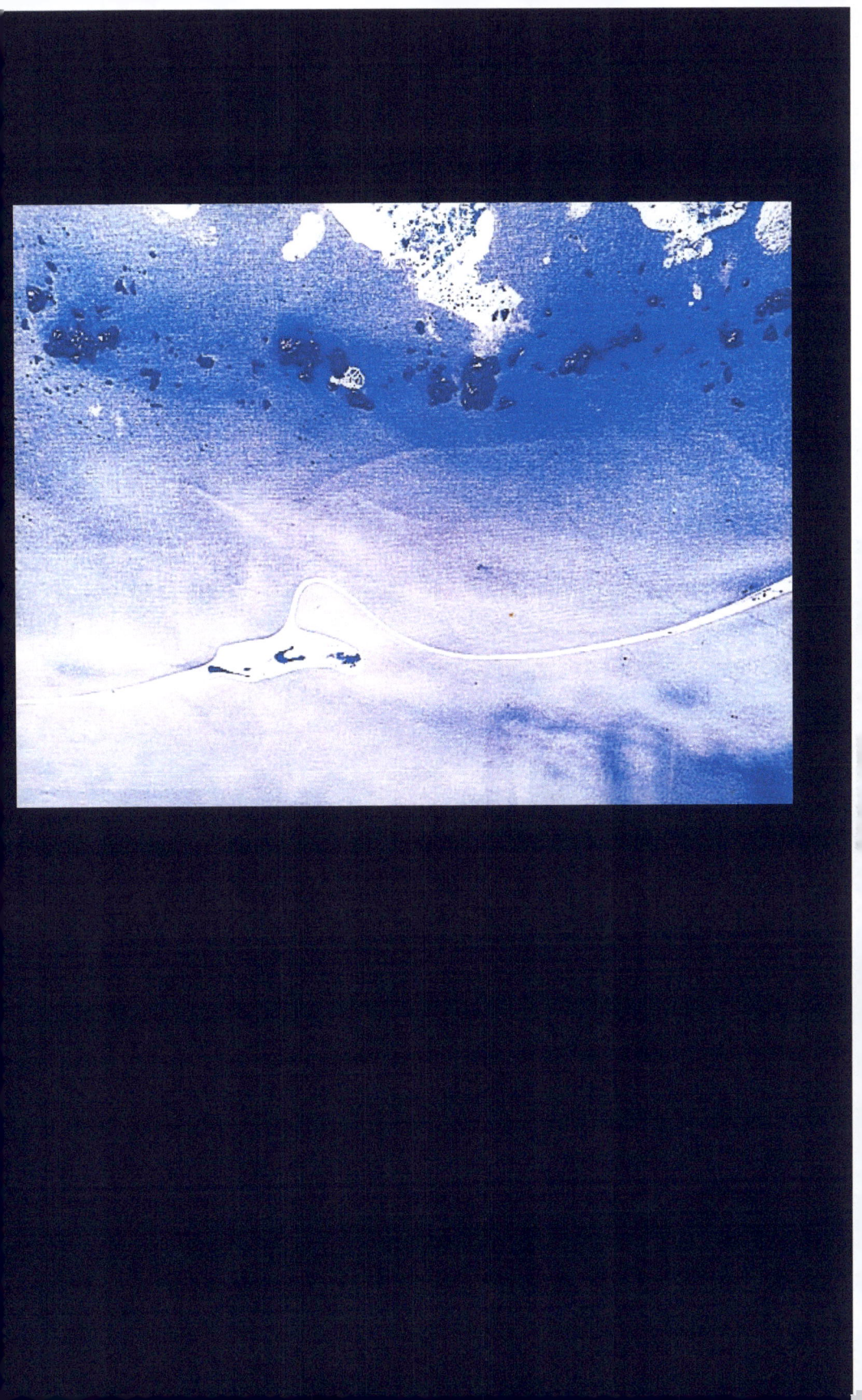

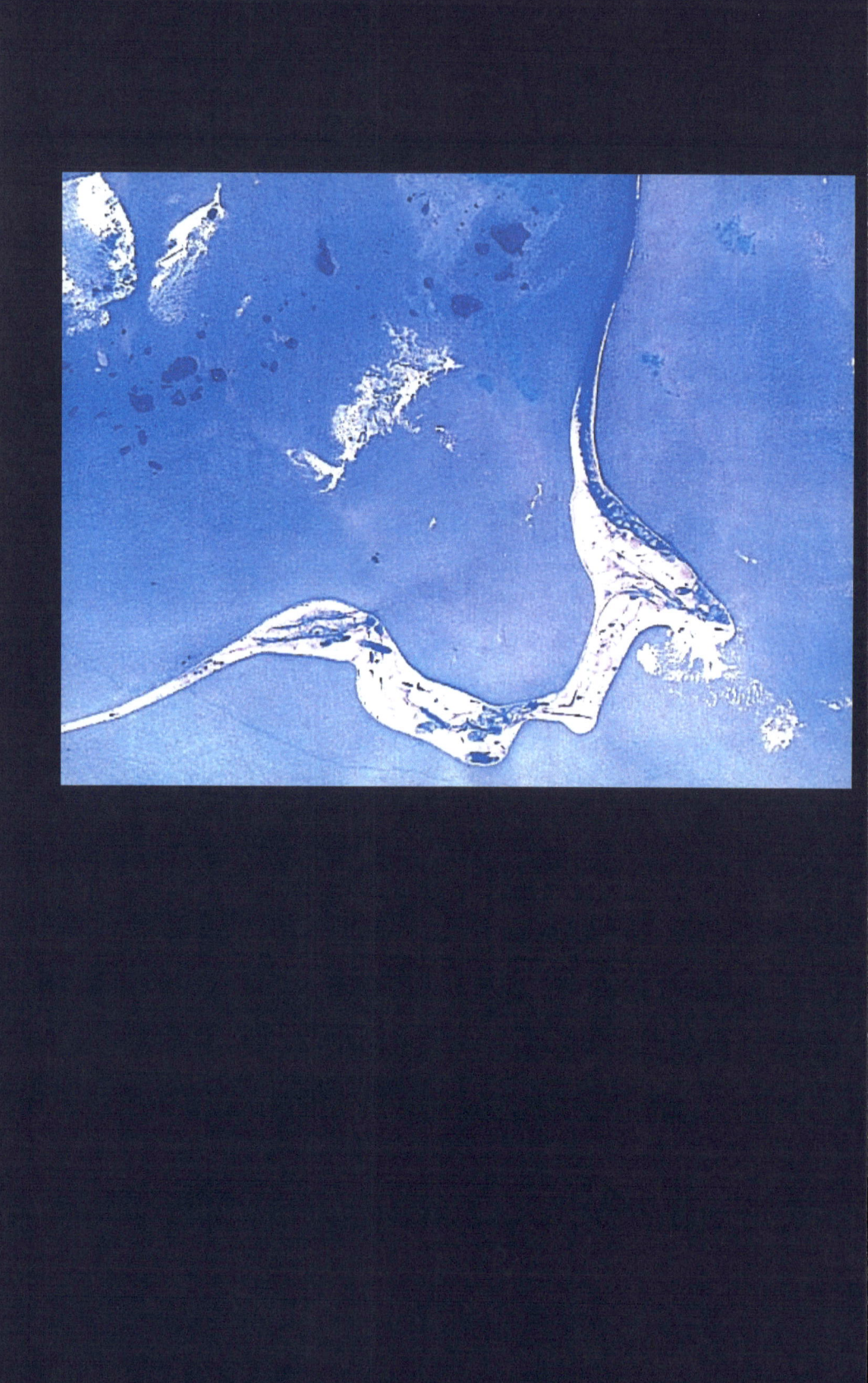

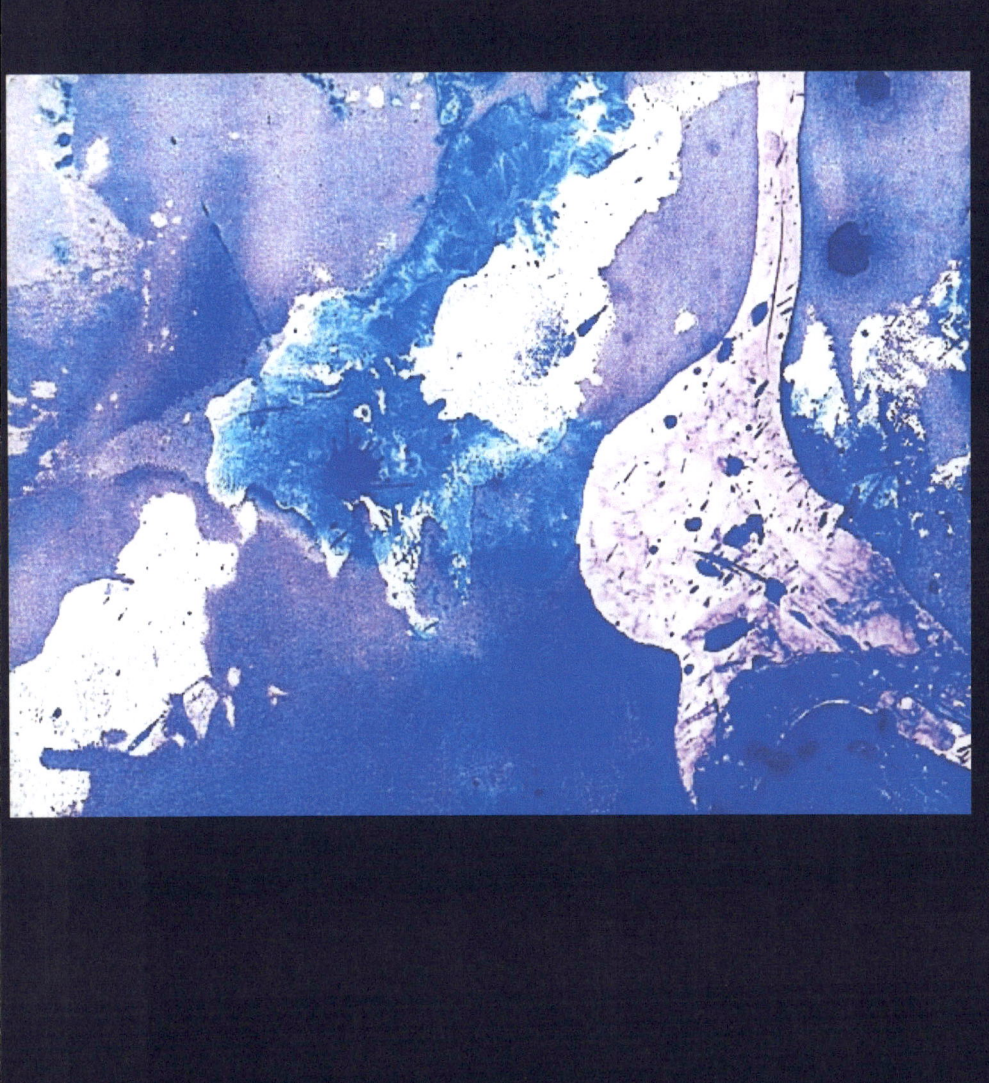

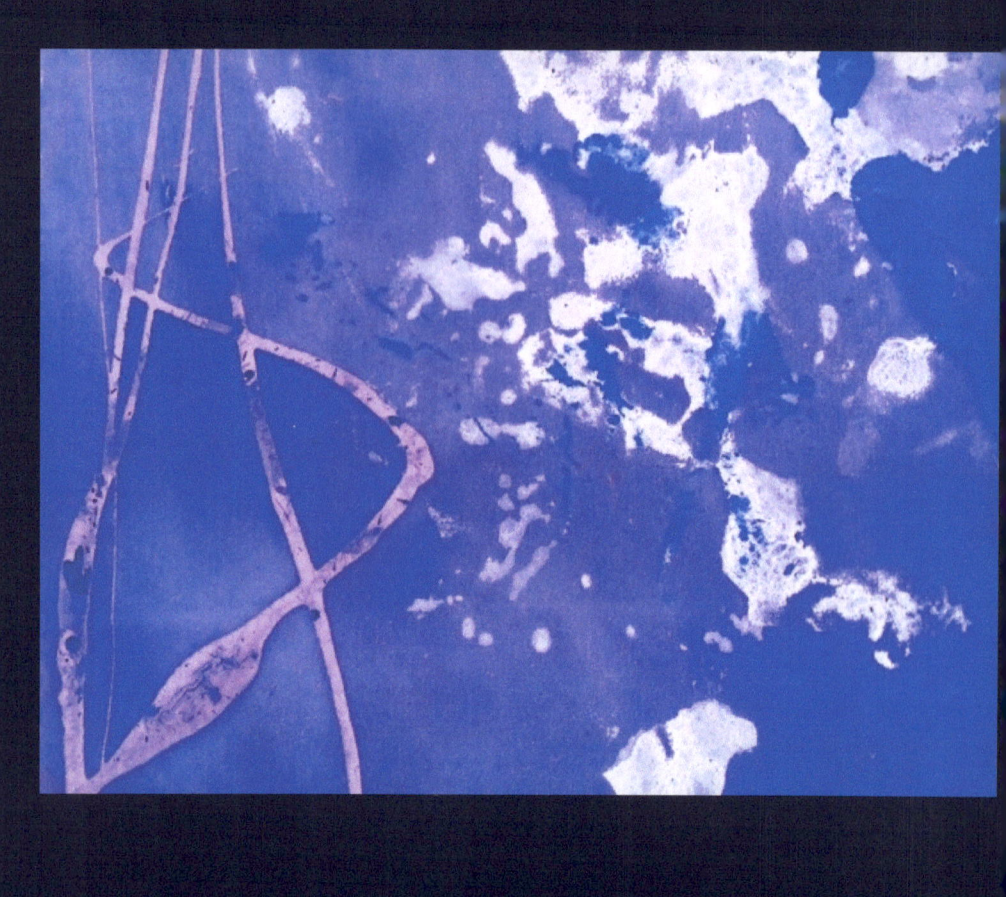

Tsunami reaches a coastal city

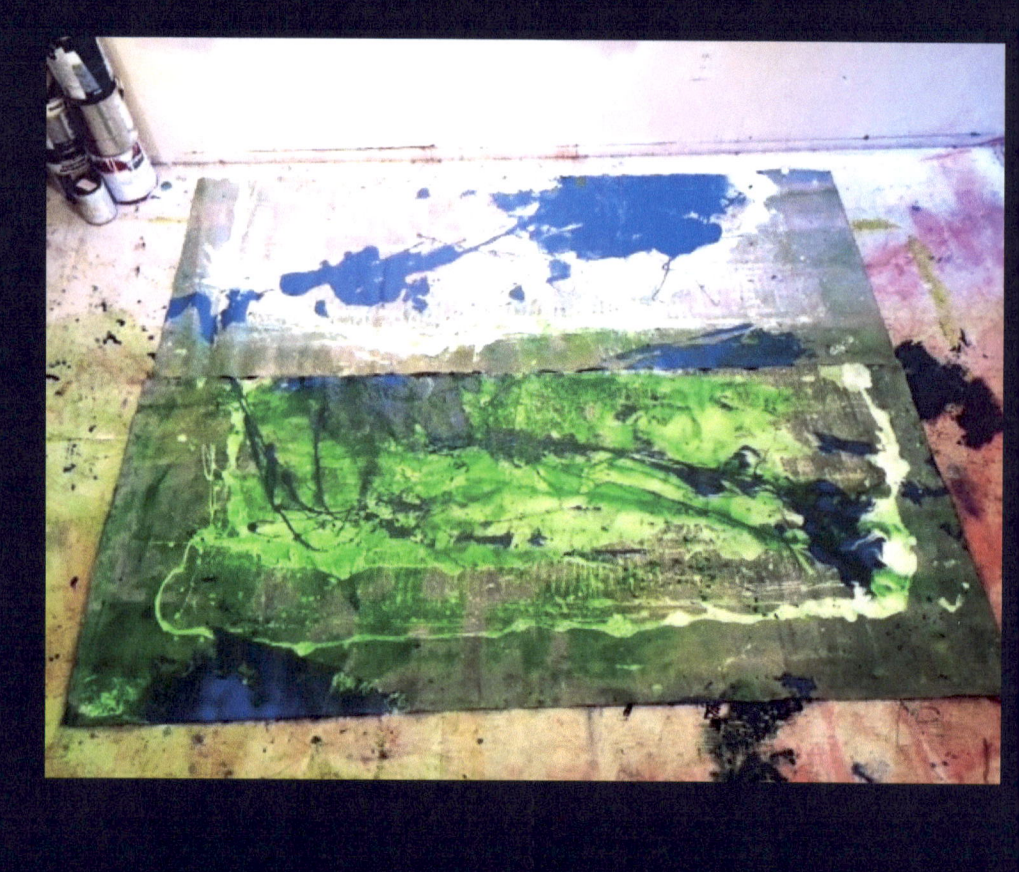

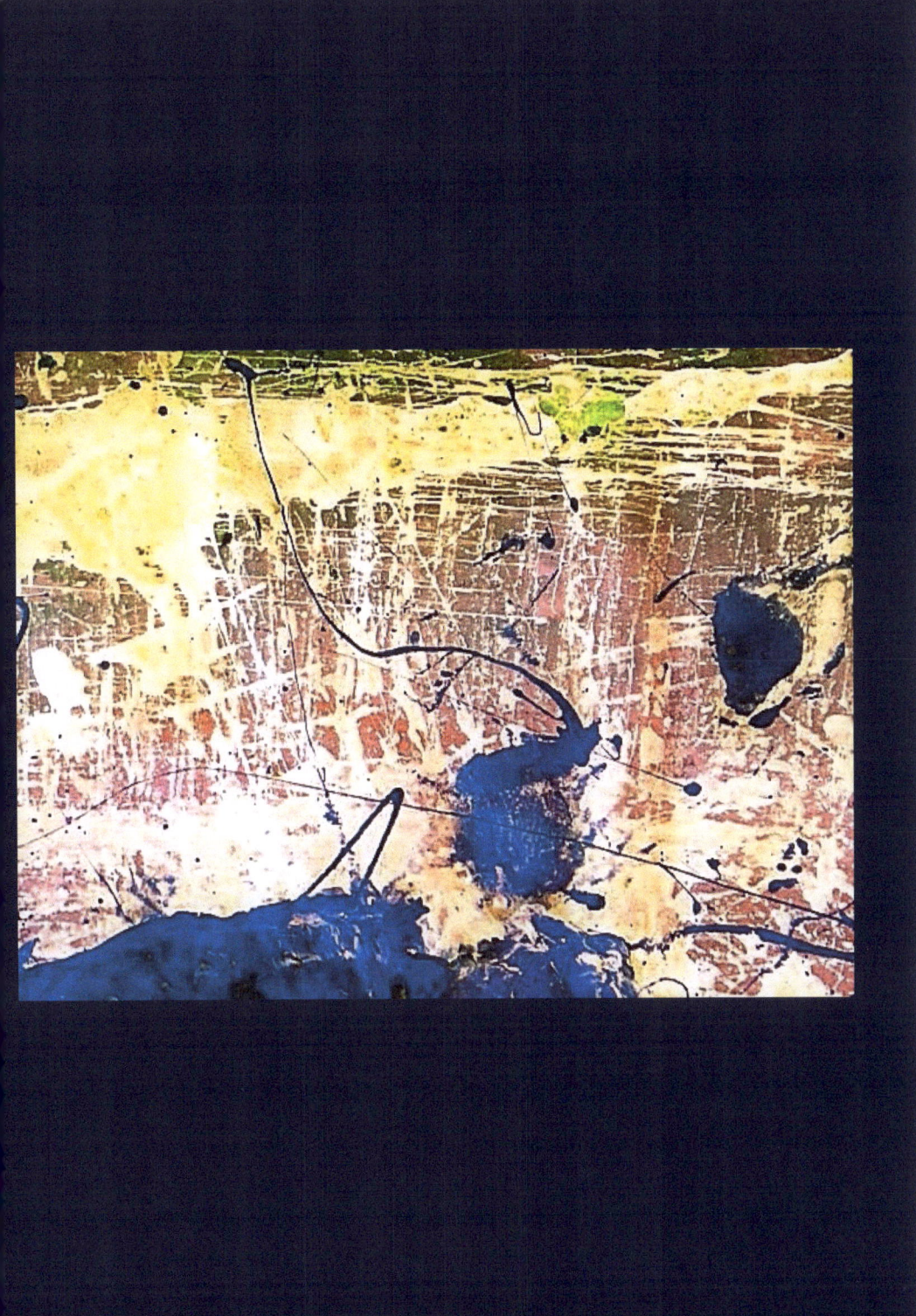

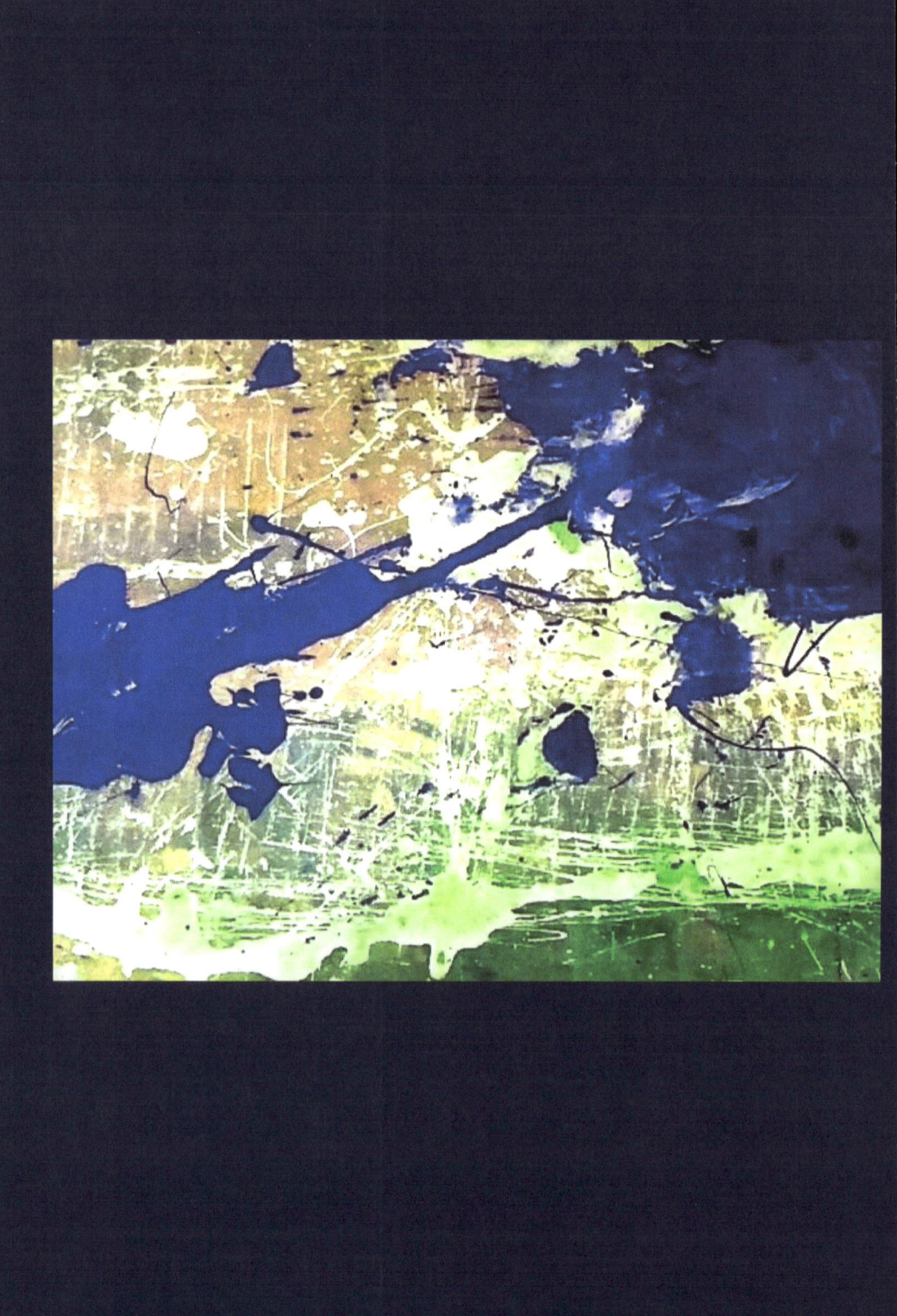

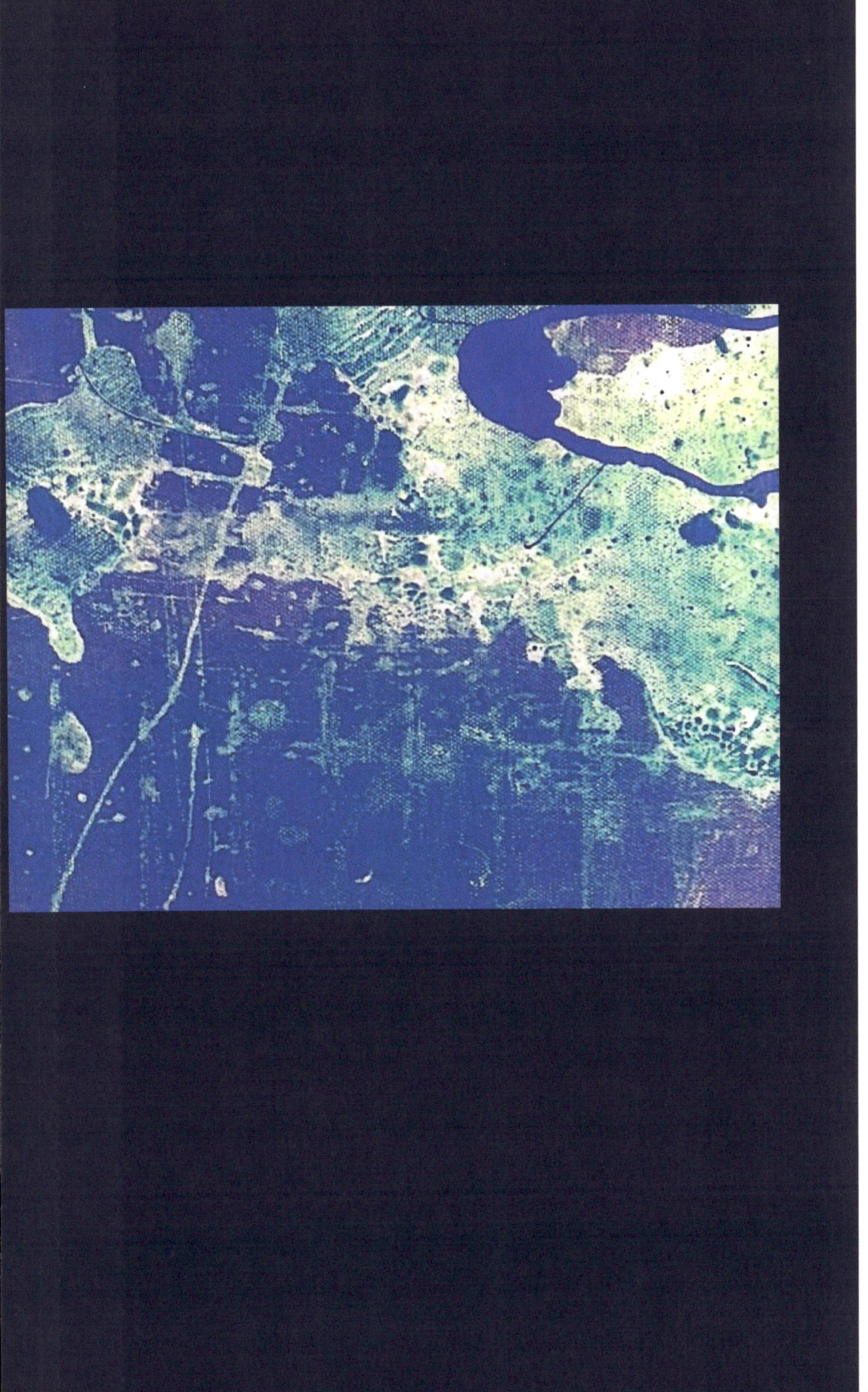

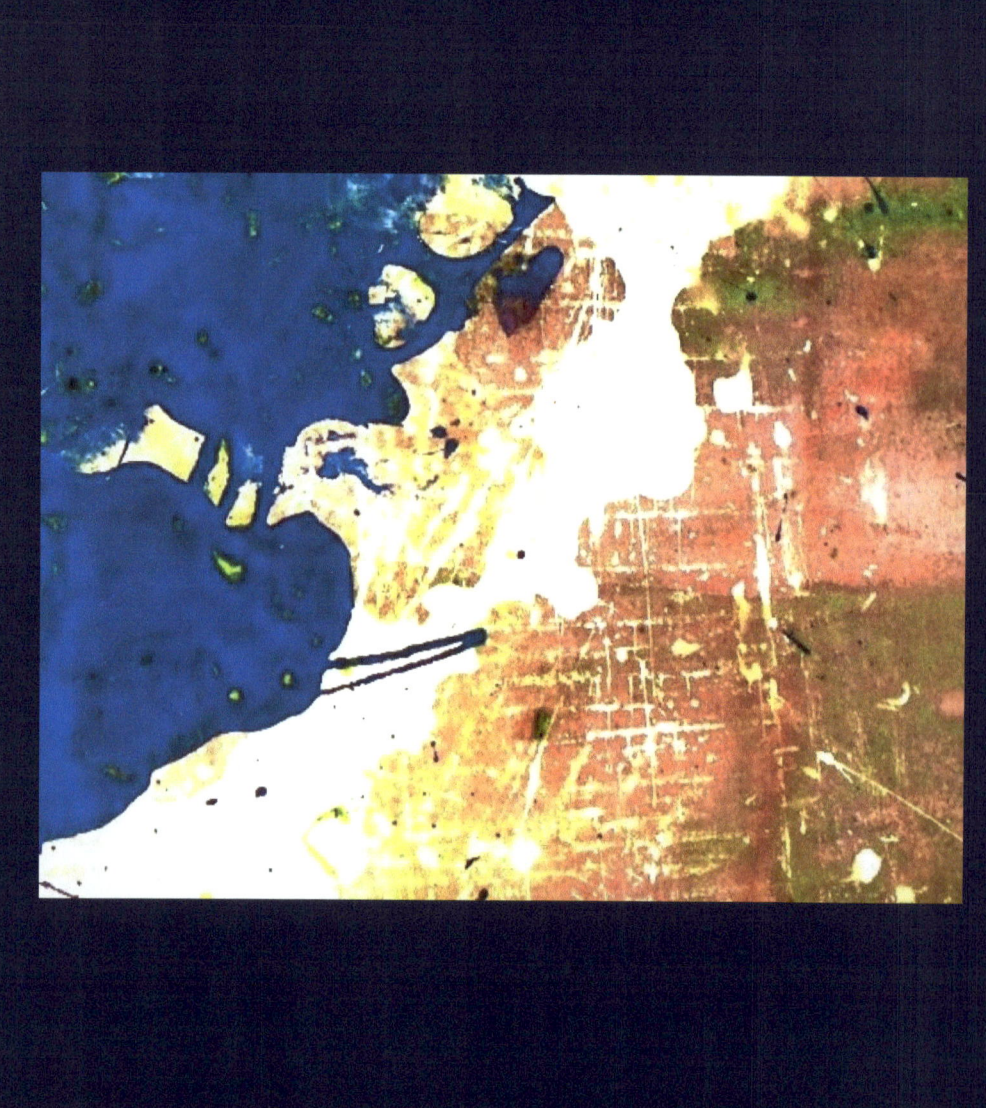

Pollution sifts through the atmosphere

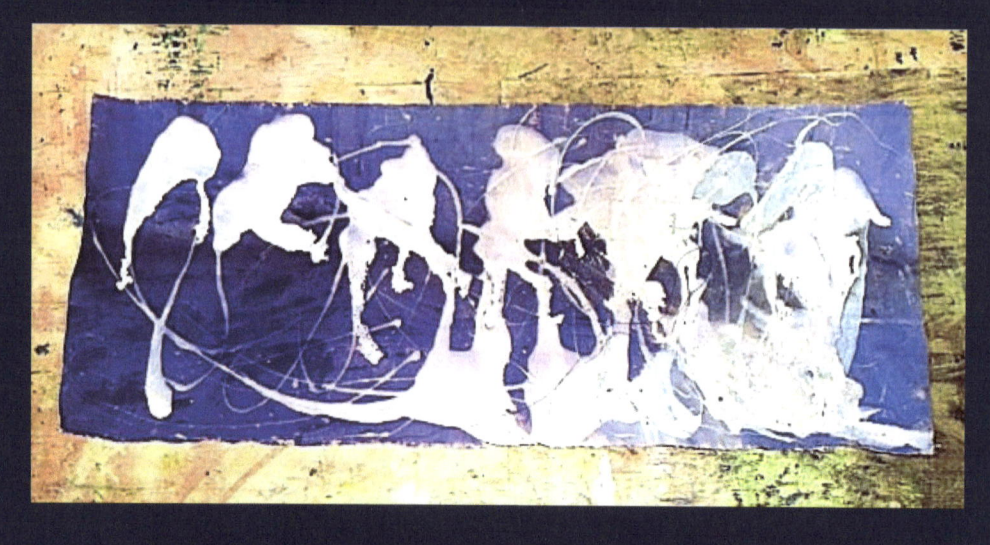

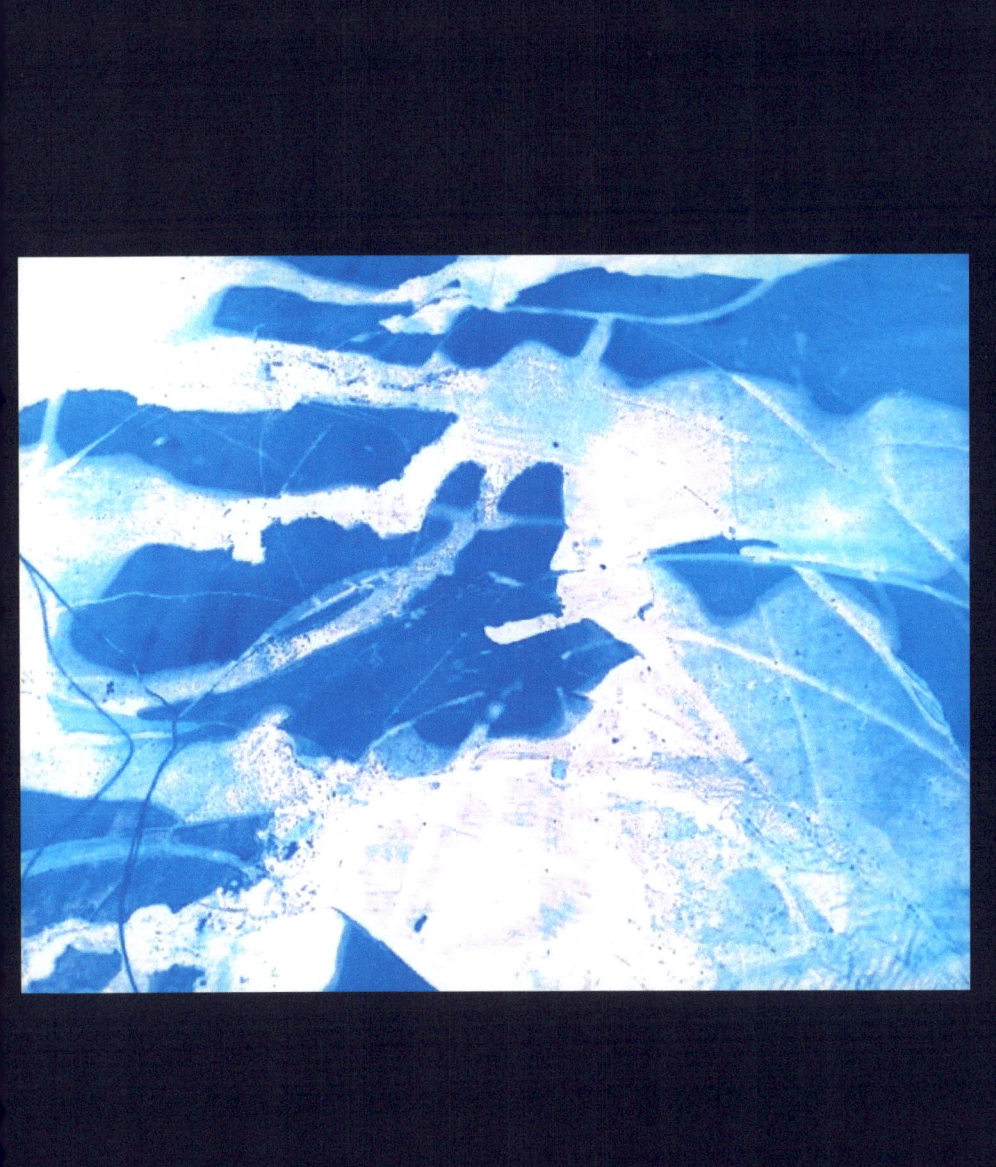

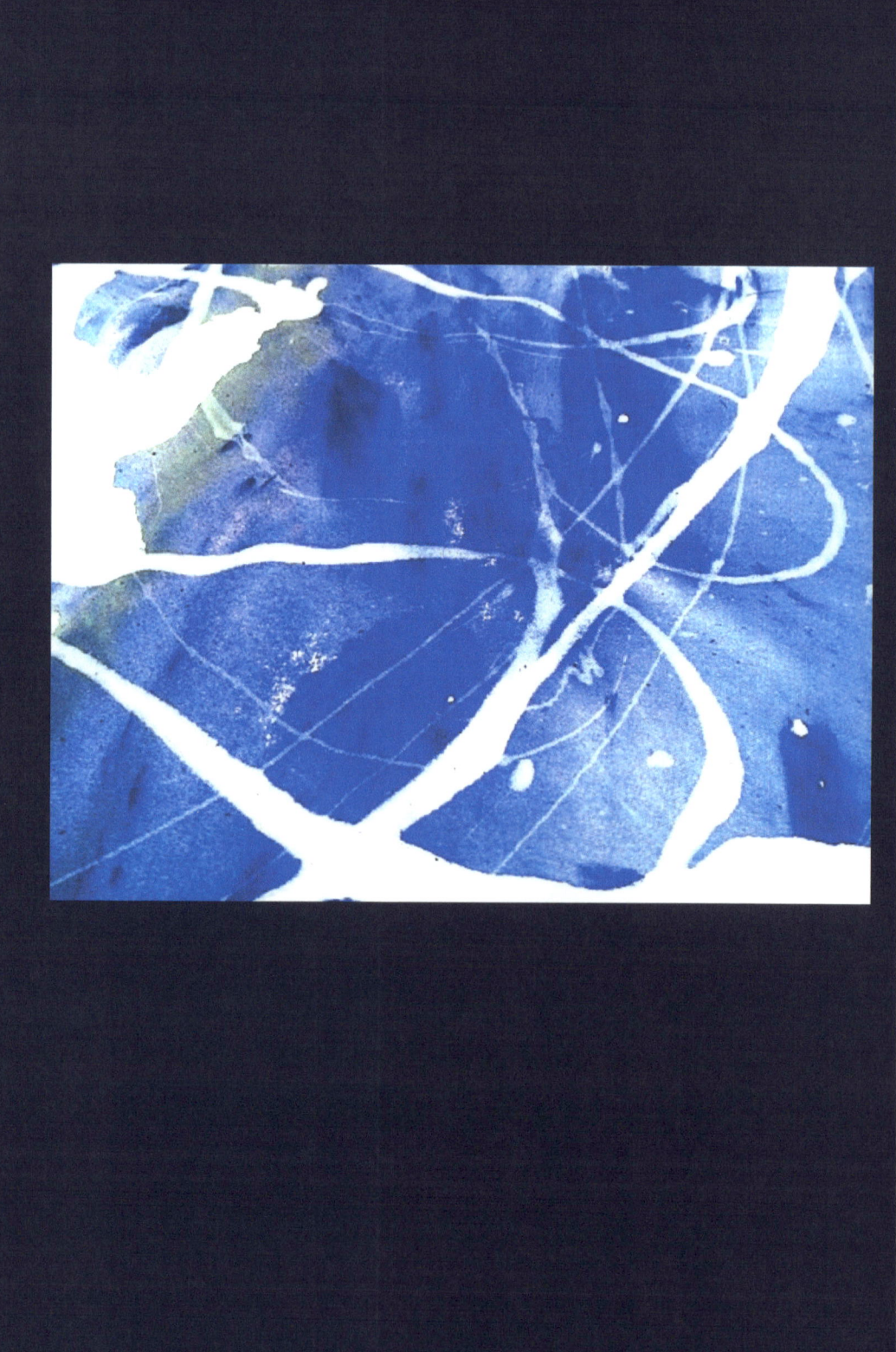

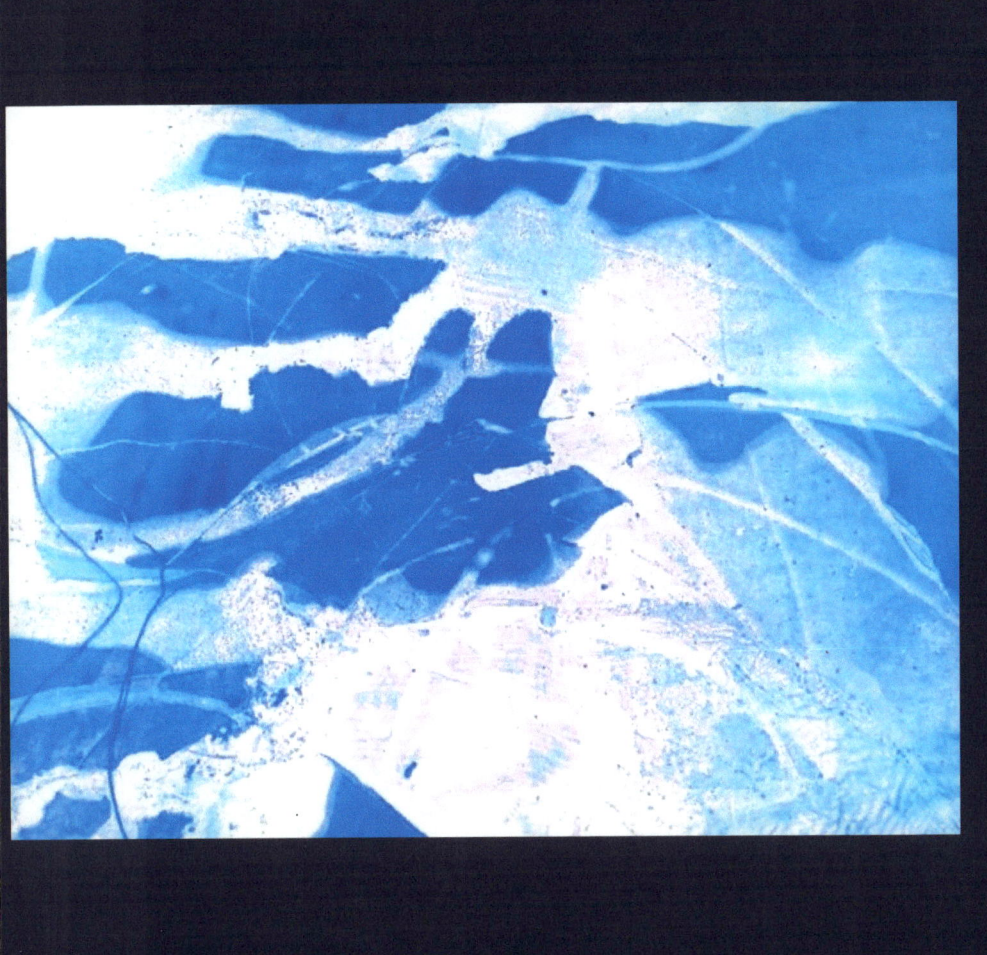

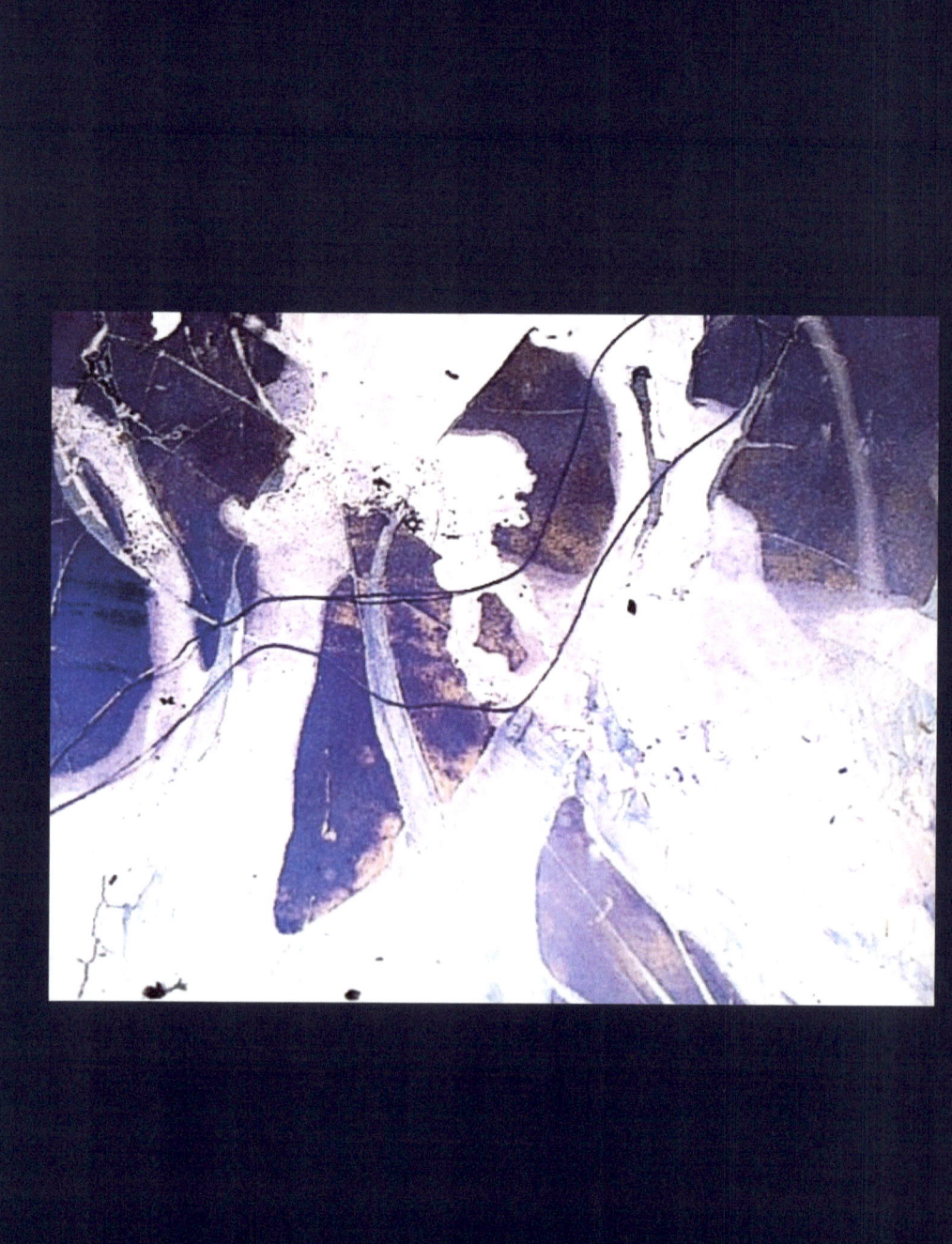

Oil spills into a city

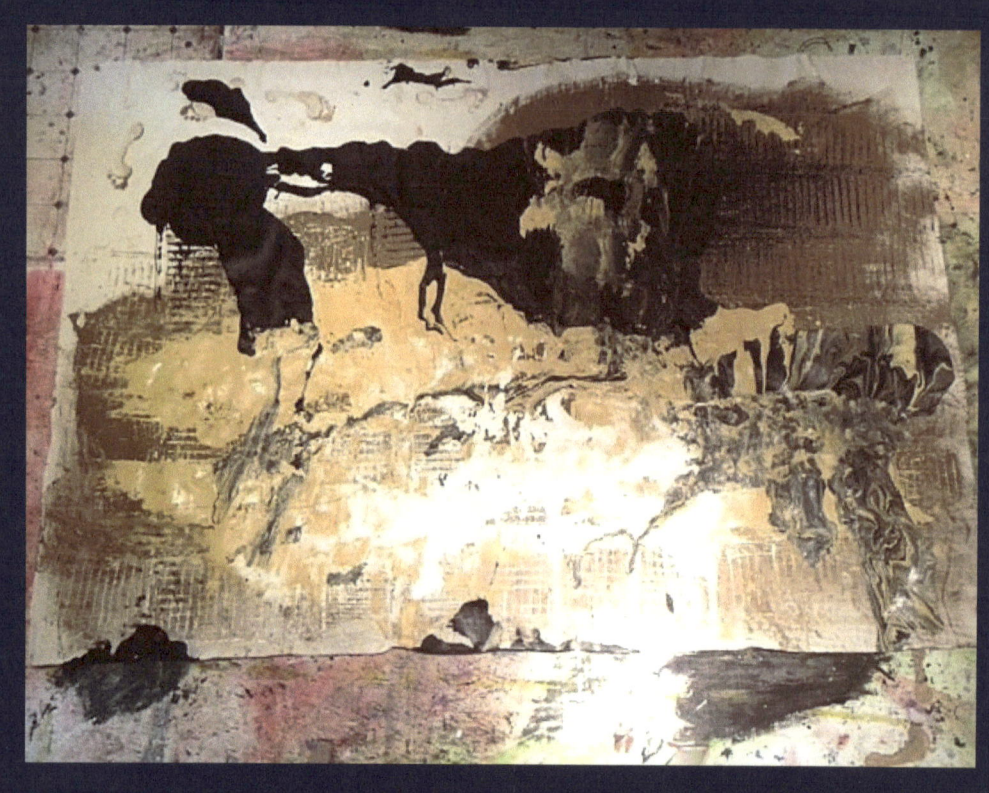

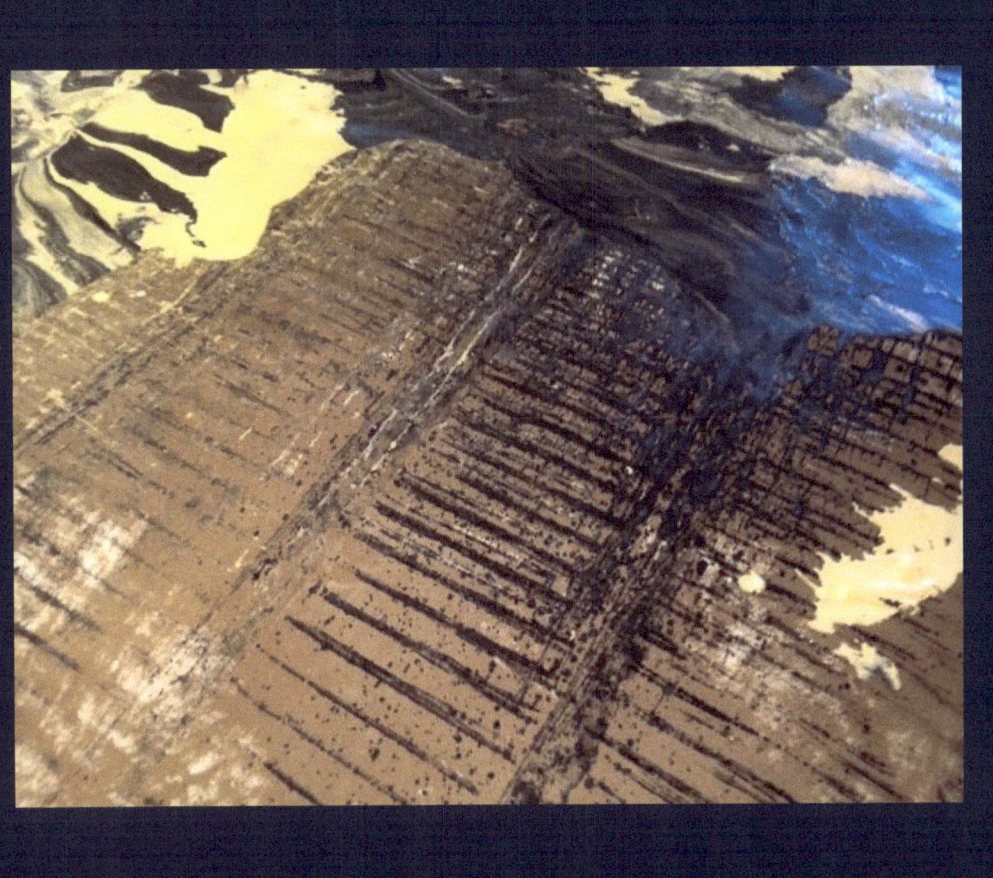

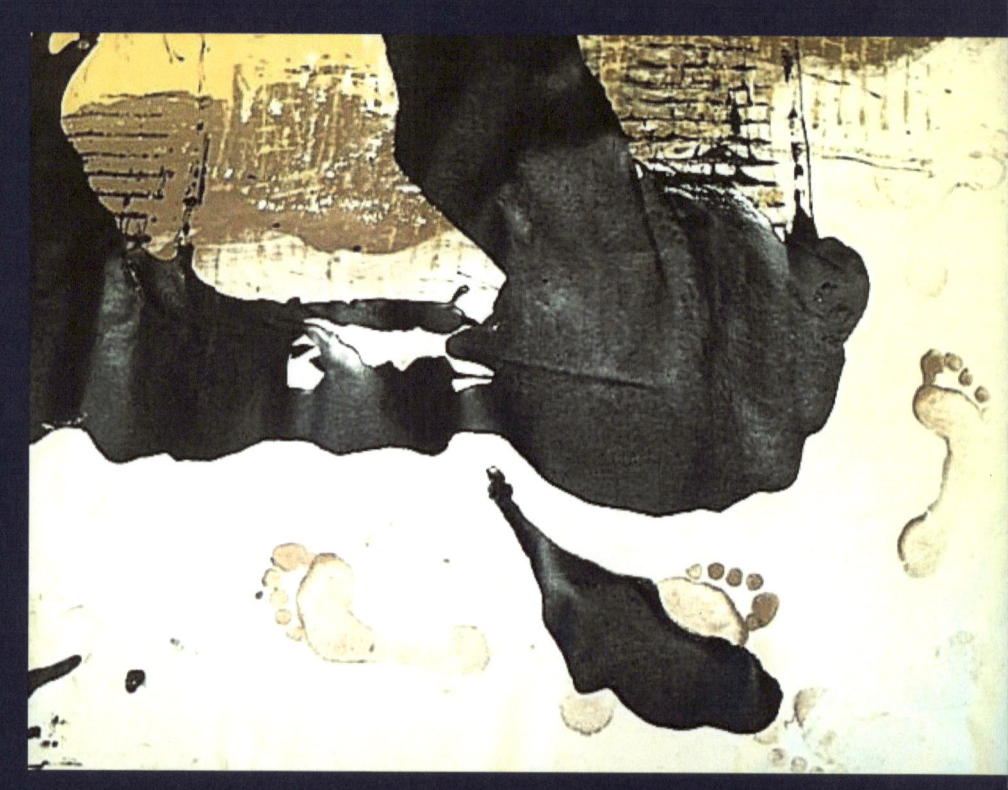

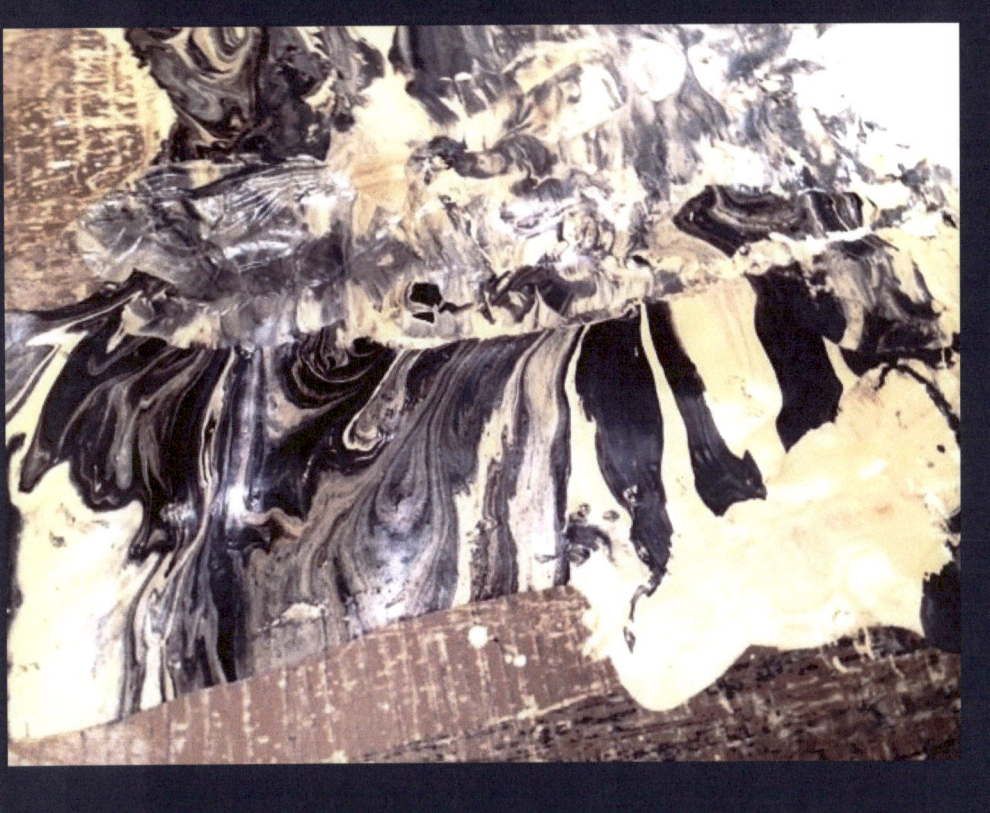

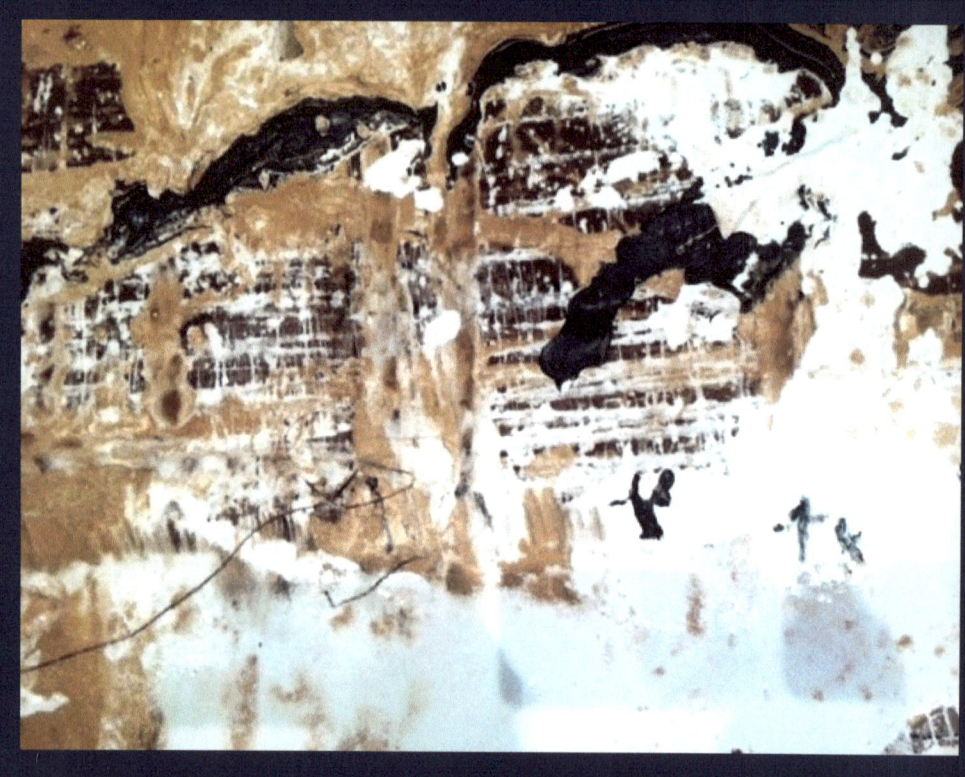

Rivers run red with blood and toxins

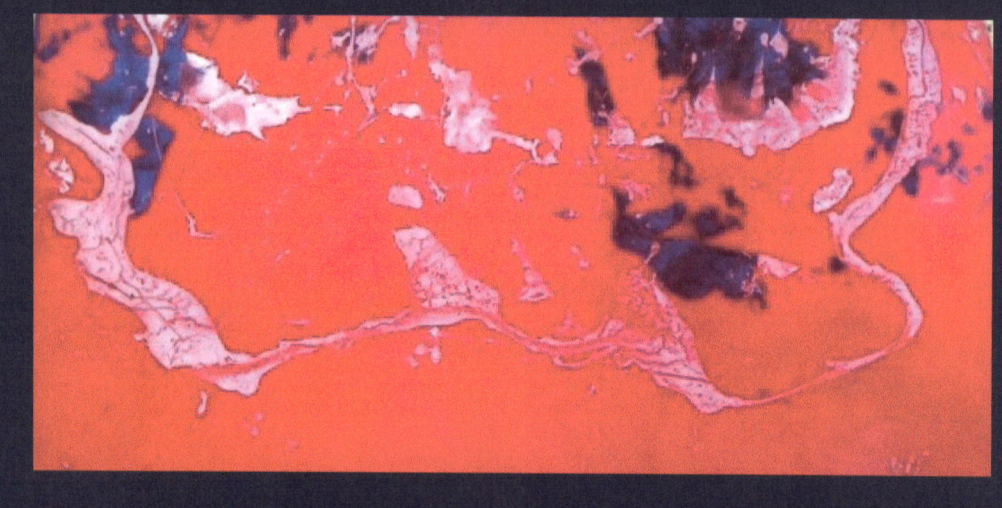

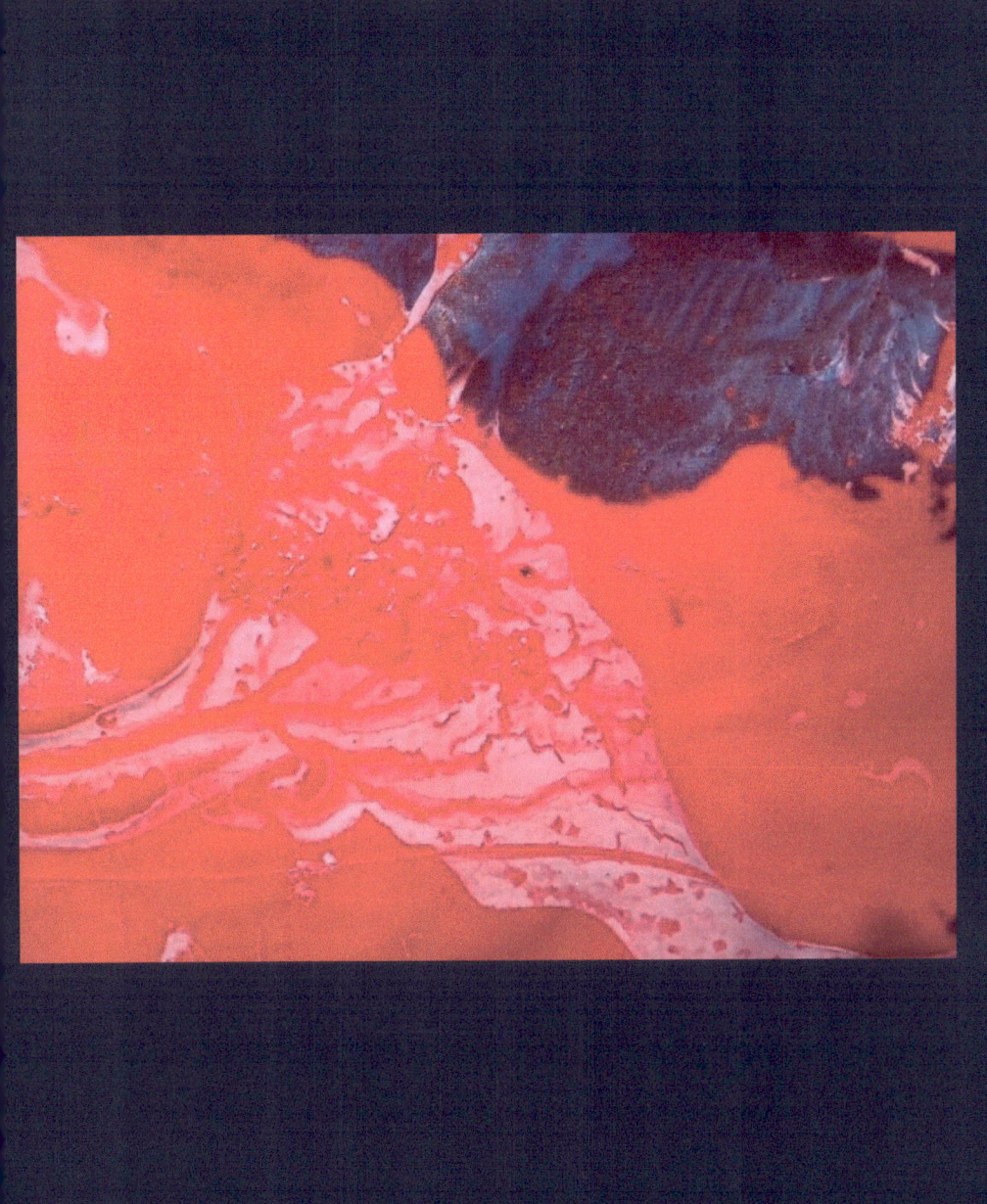

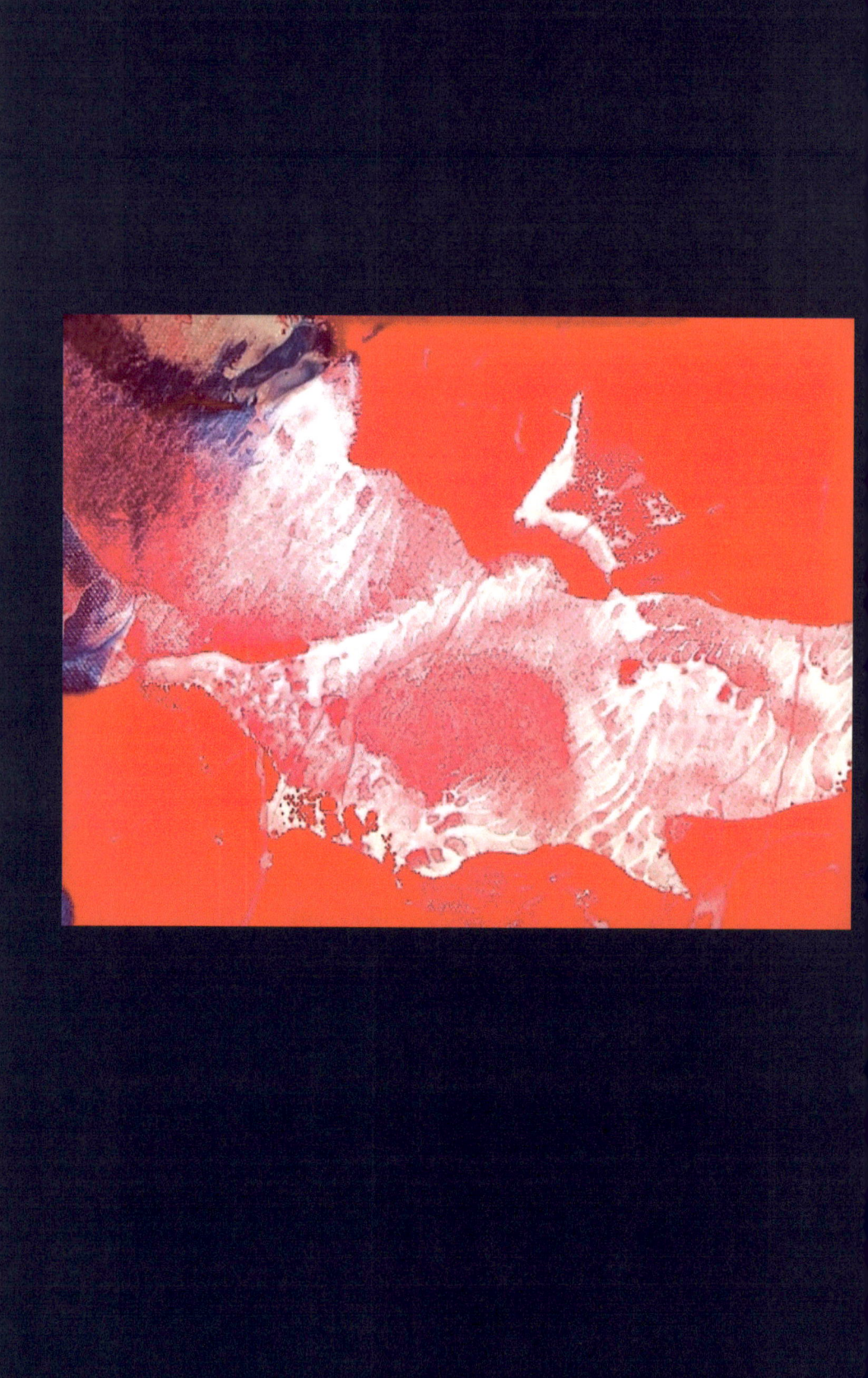

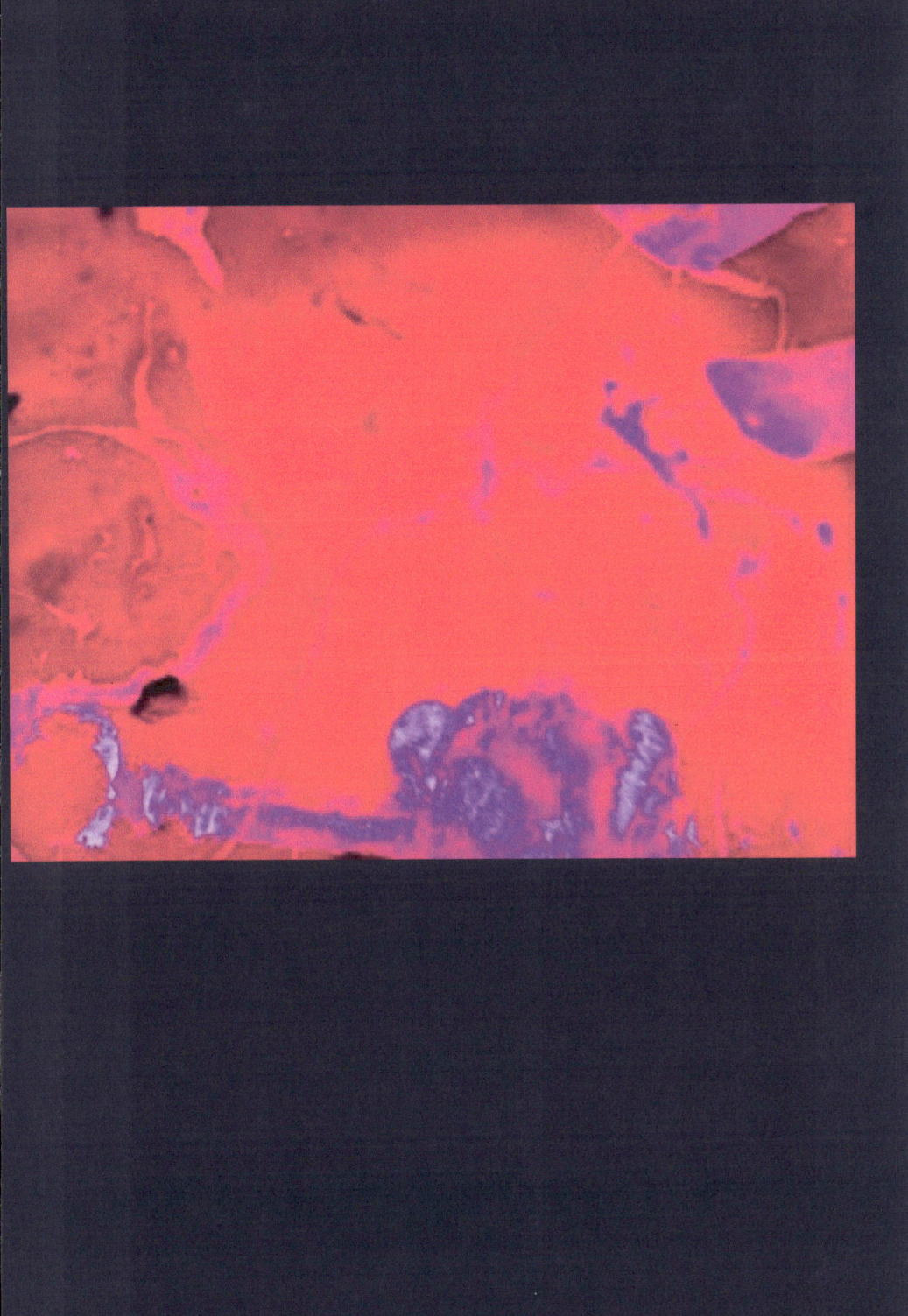

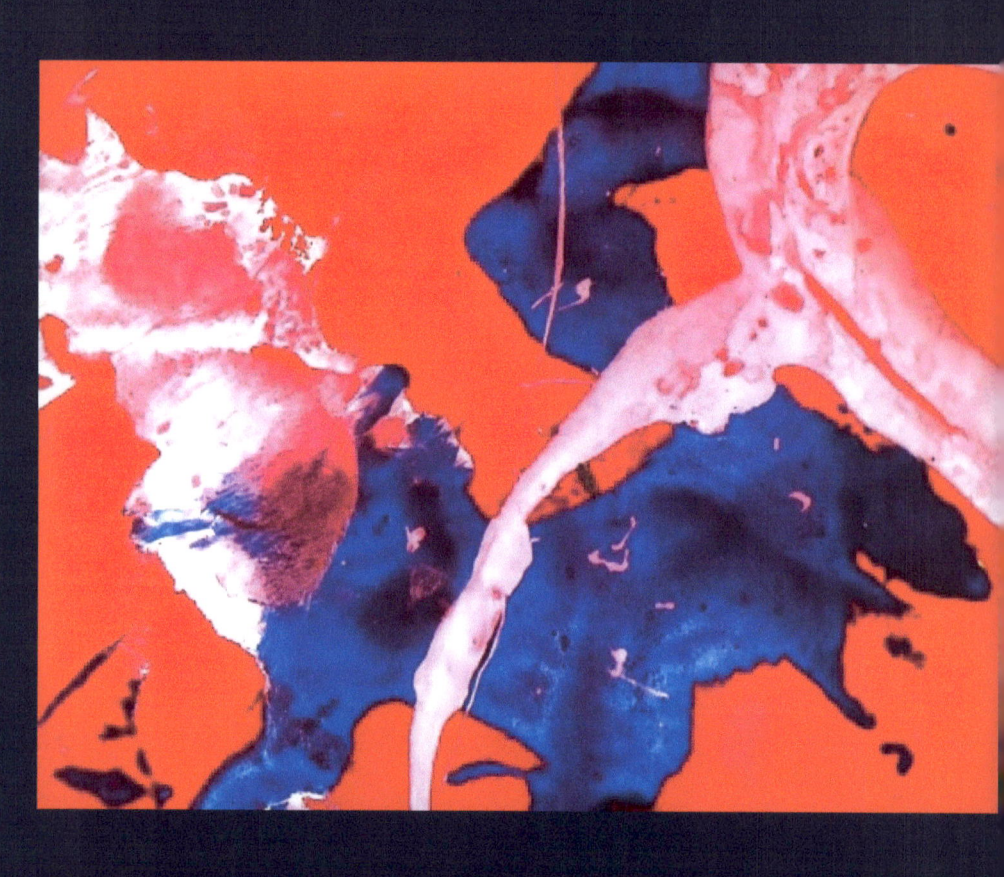

The Great Pacific

Garbage Patch

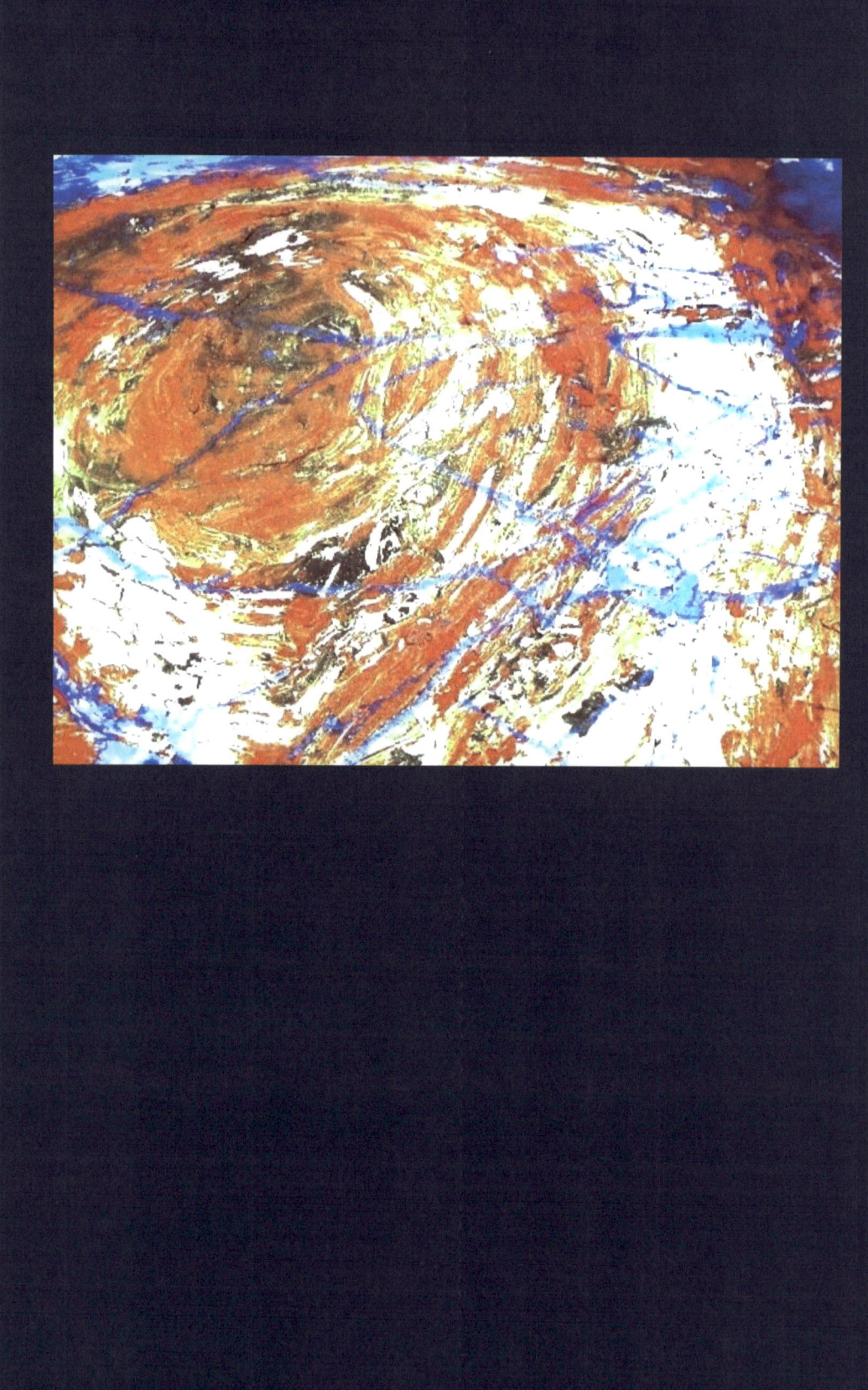

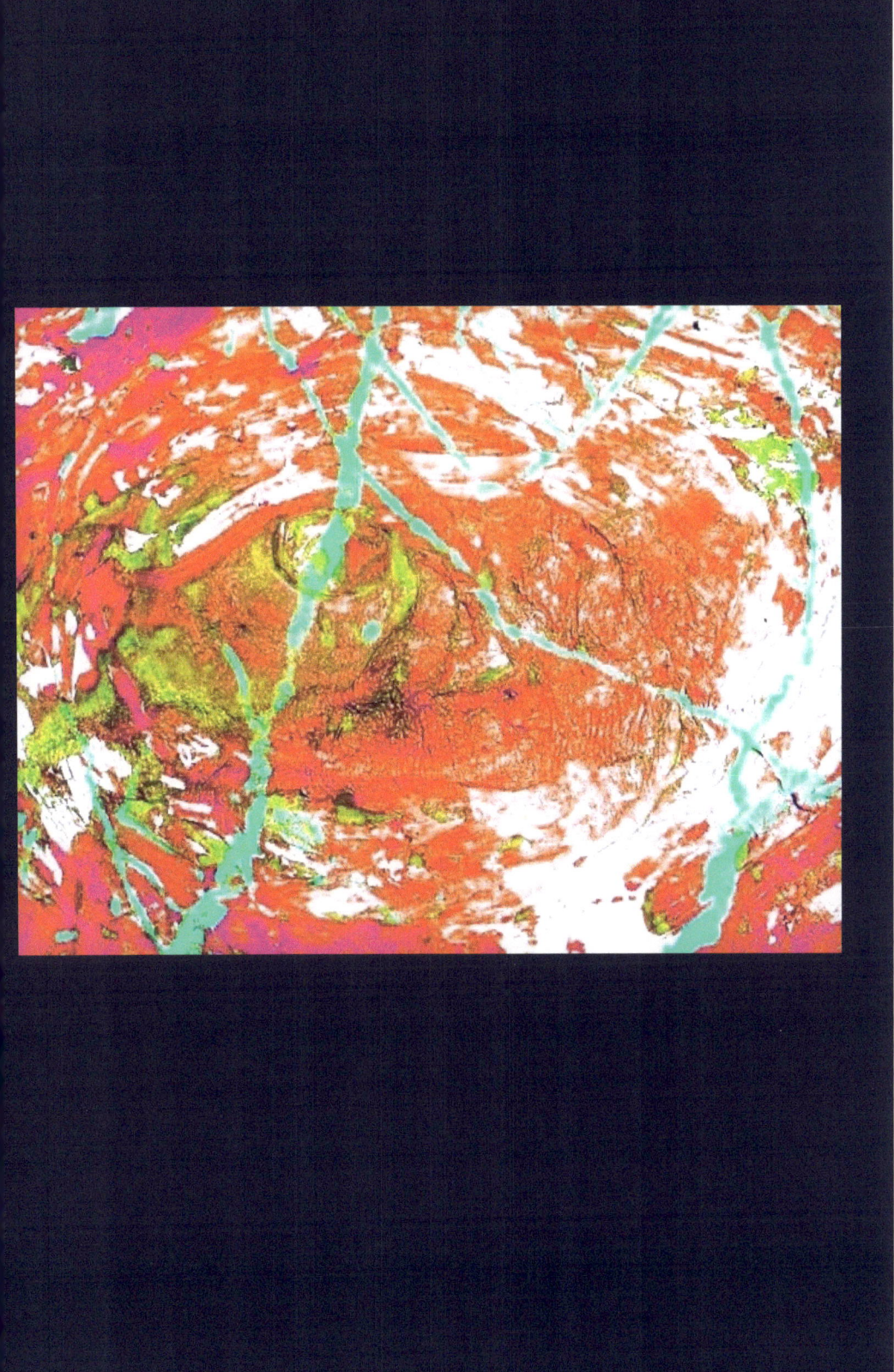

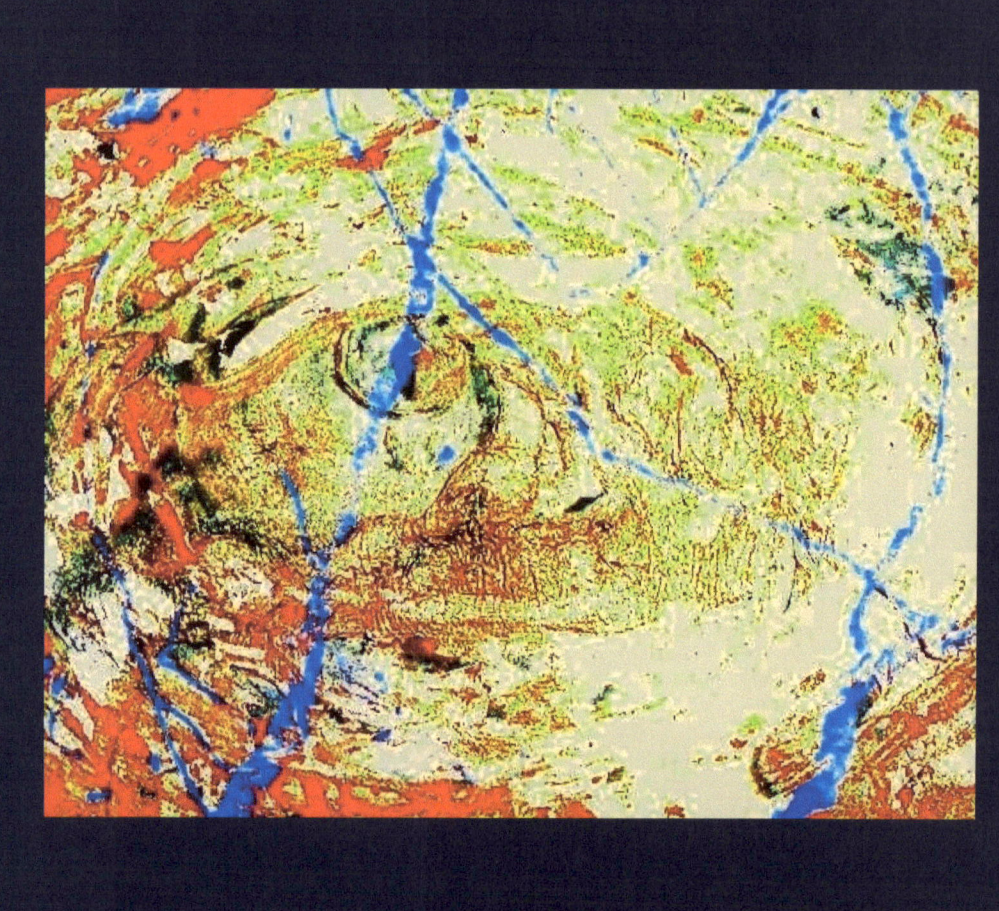

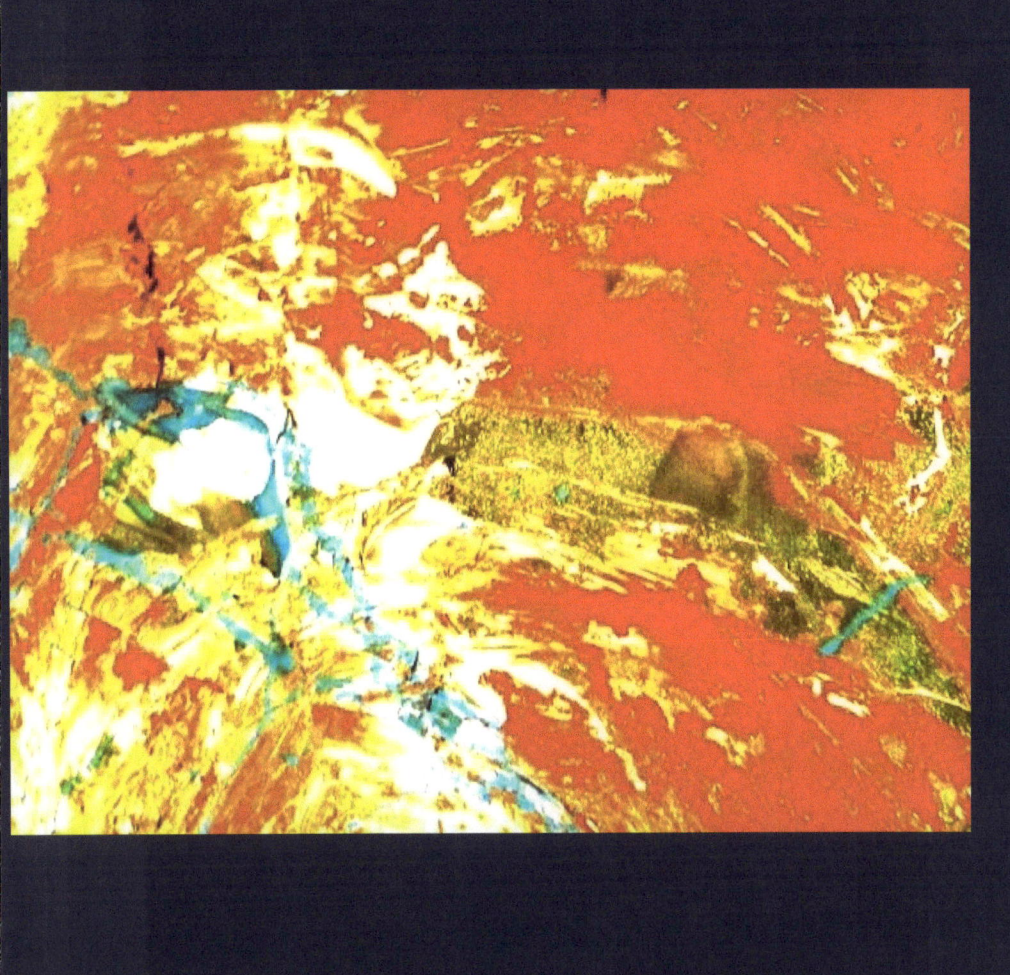

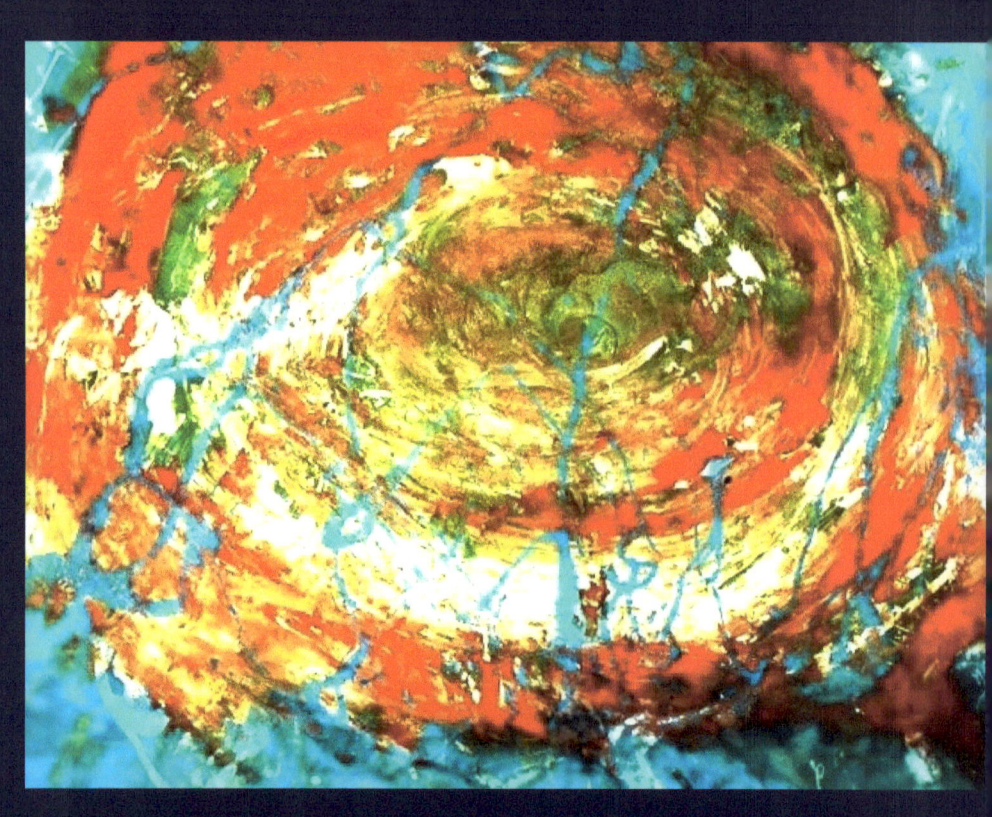

The Cascadia Fault ruptures

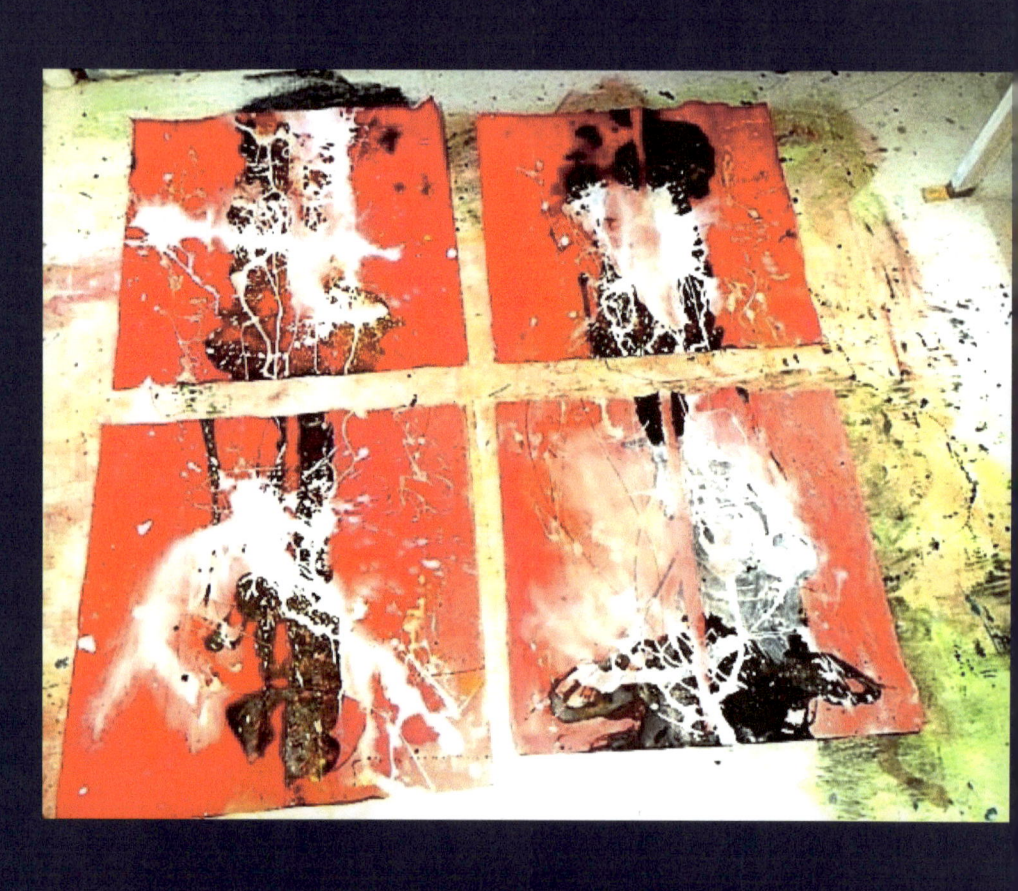

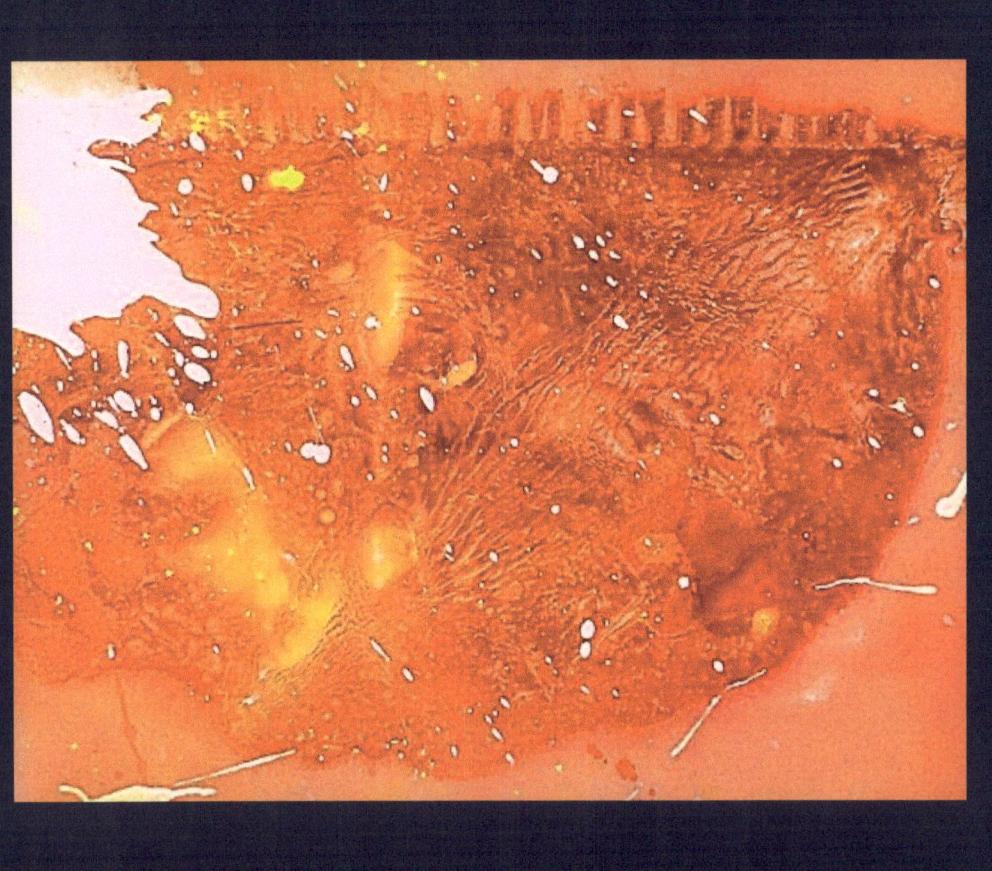

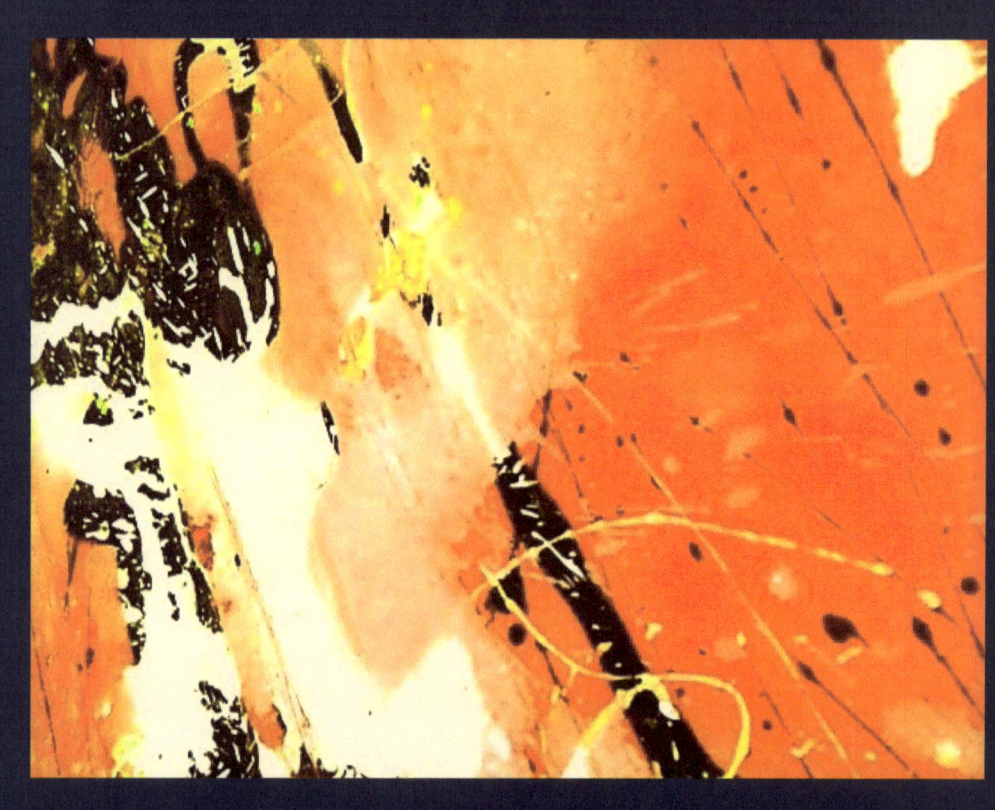

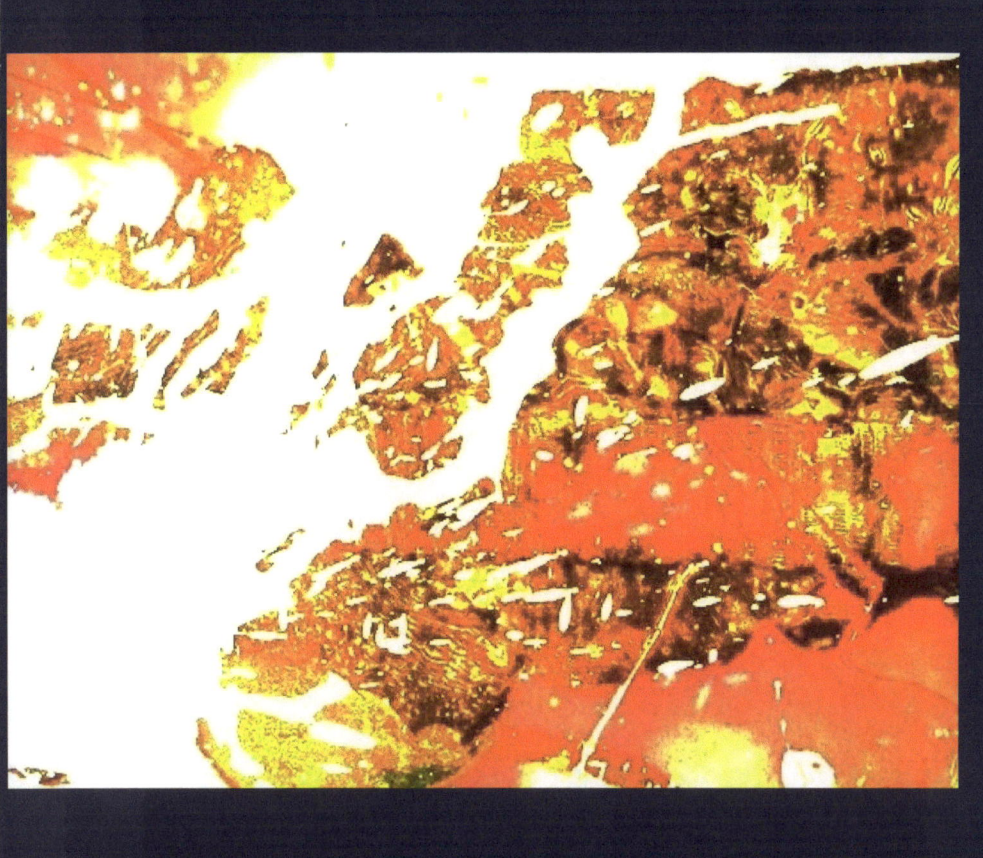

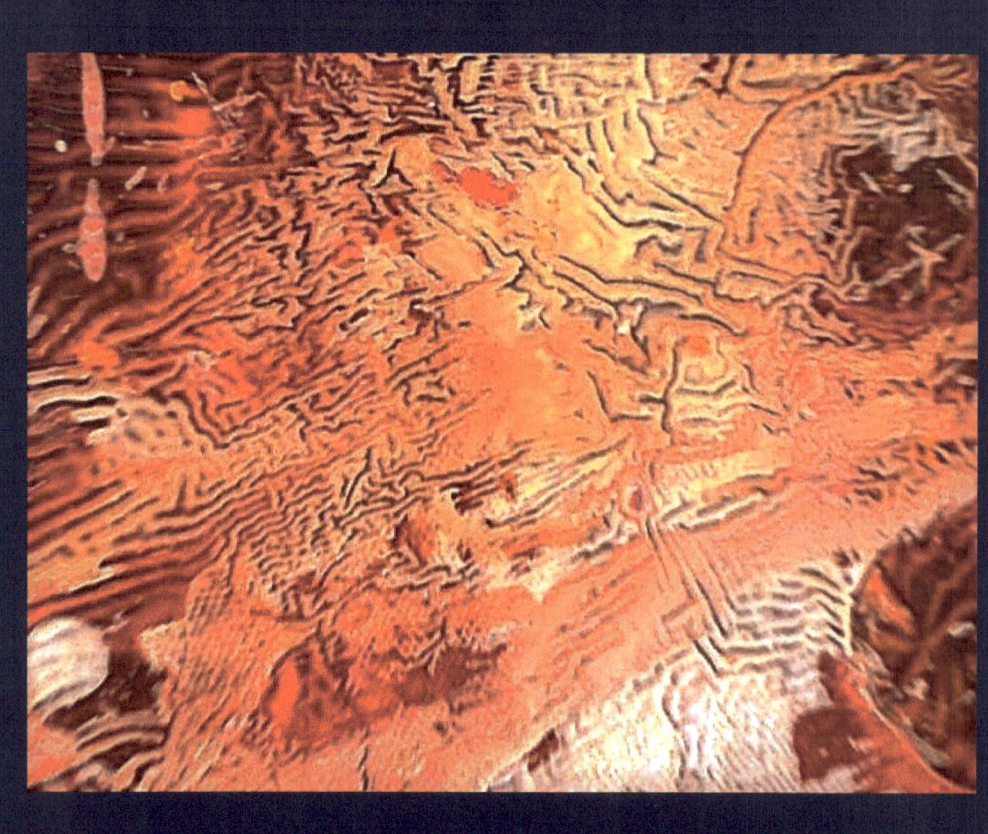

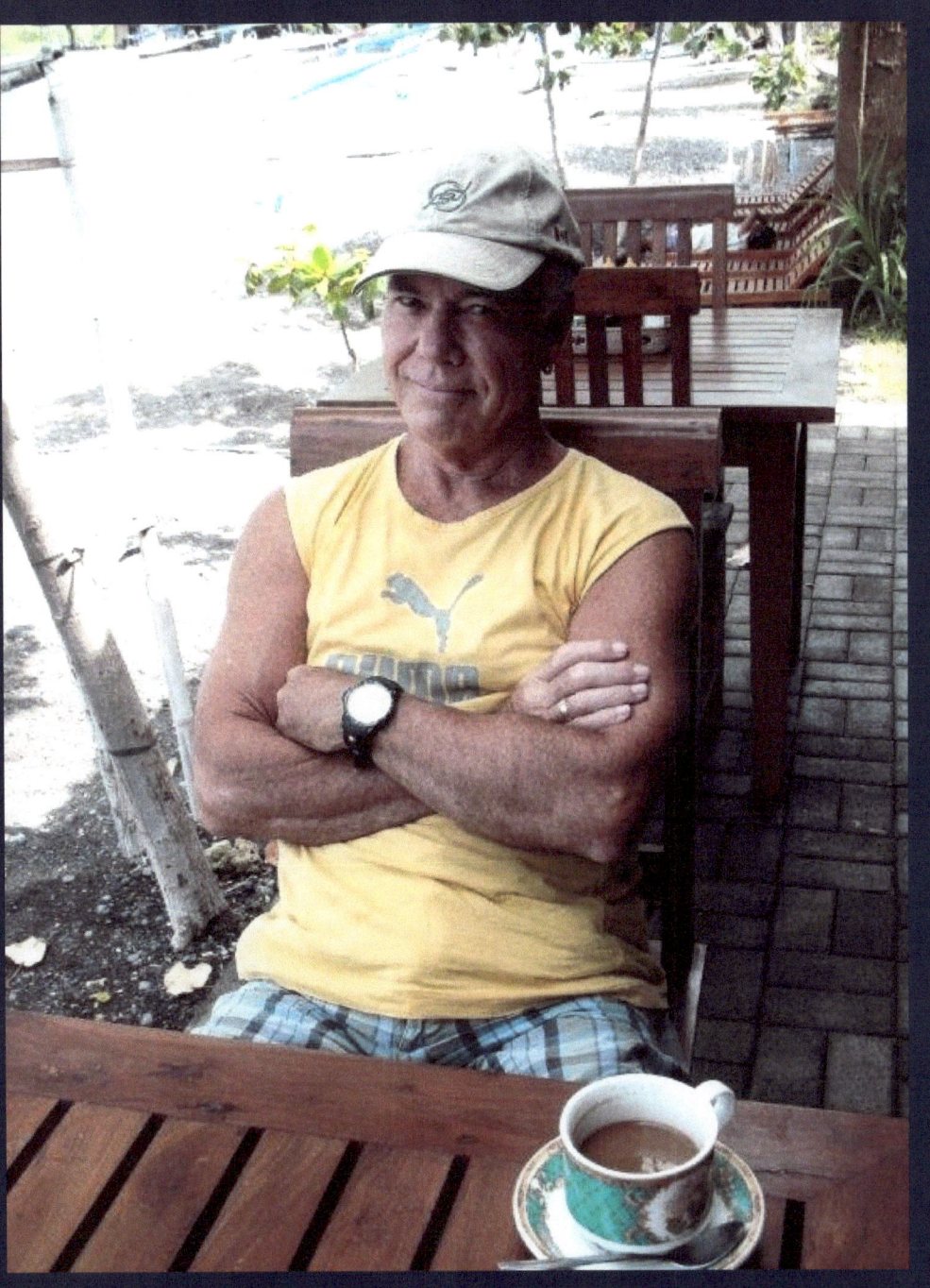

Gary Walters received a B.A. in Romance Languages and Literature and an M.F. A. and Ph.D. in Art and Archeology from Princeton University. He has taught at McGill, Concordia, and Carleton Universities and at the Institute for the Arts in Denpassar, Bali, Indonesia

" I left academe following a seduction by the Muses and so have maintained a studio and written books, mostly poetry, for the past 25 years. I live alone because my partner, Peter, has late stage dementia. Witnessing this has increased my sense that the whole human race is coming down with a dementia. The paintings in this book were a big artistic challenge and they are a warning."

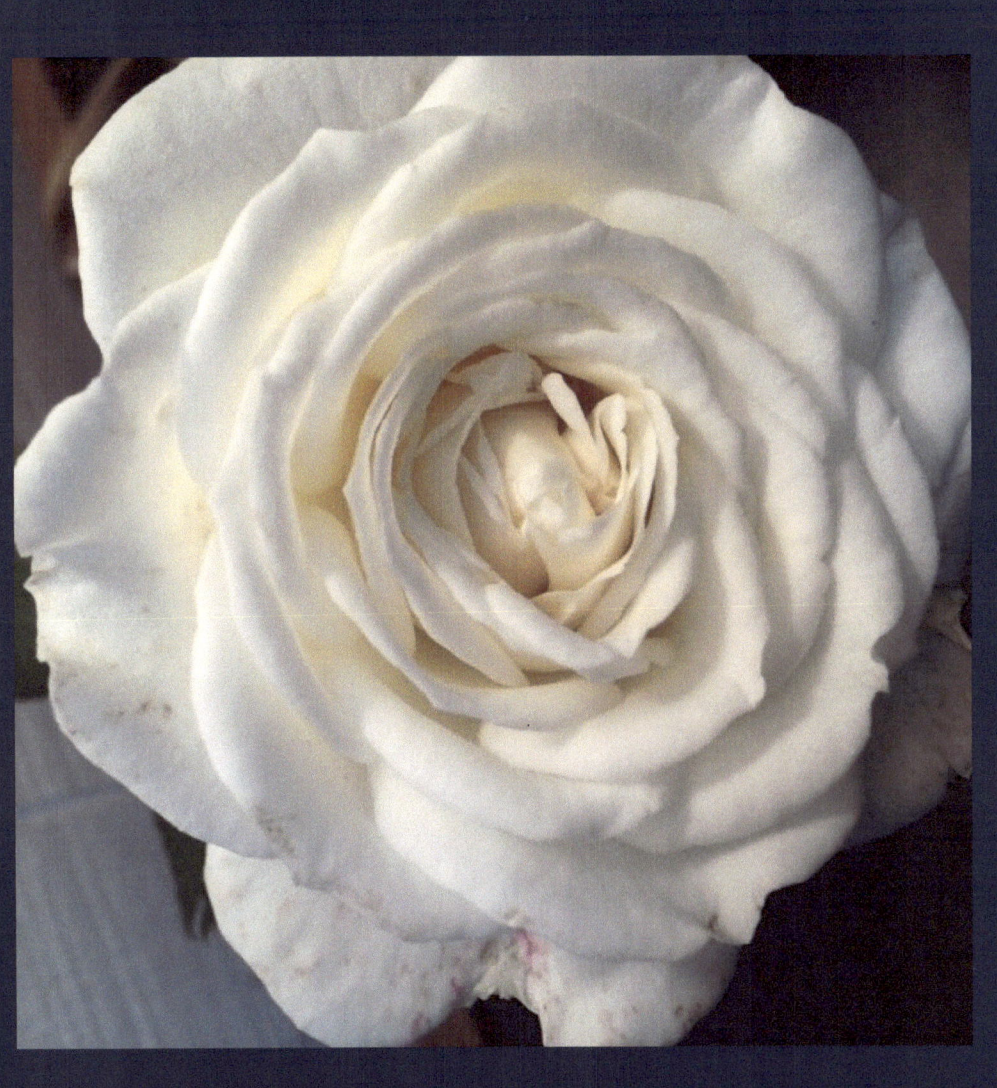

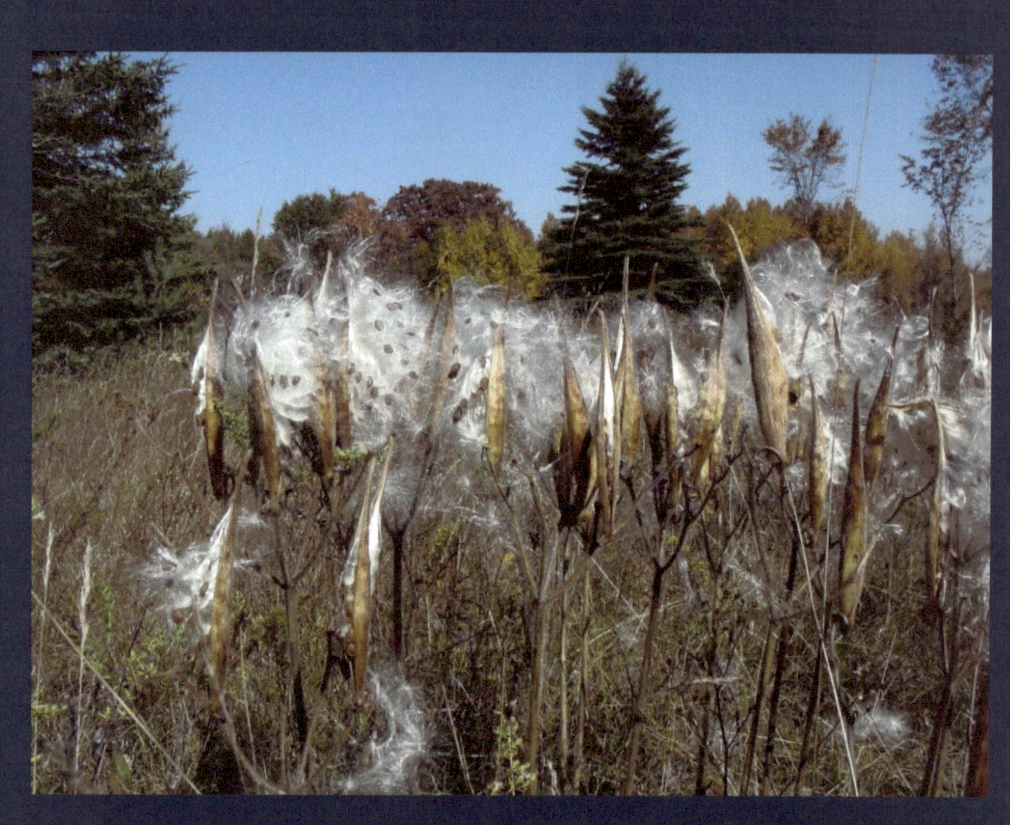

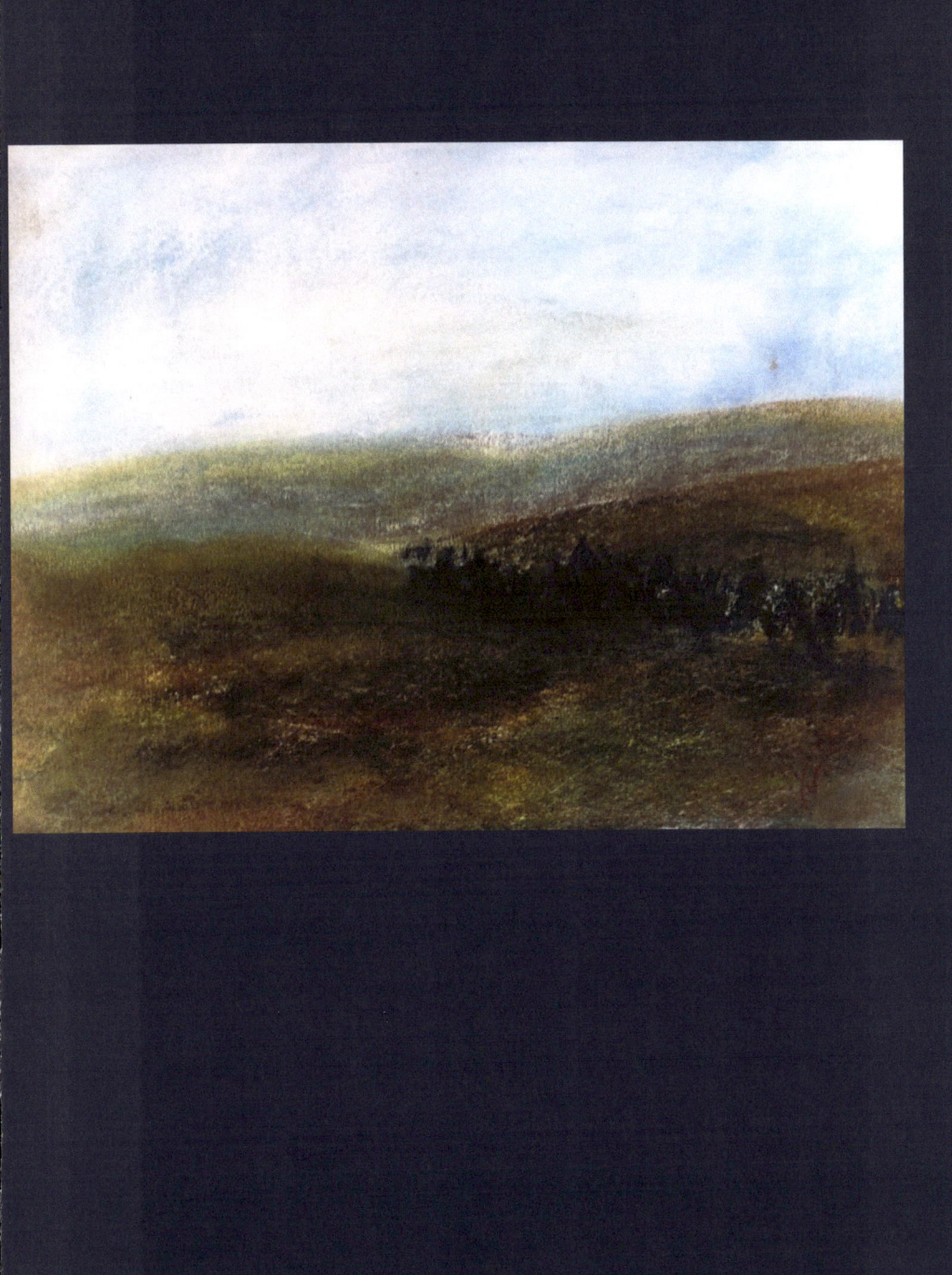

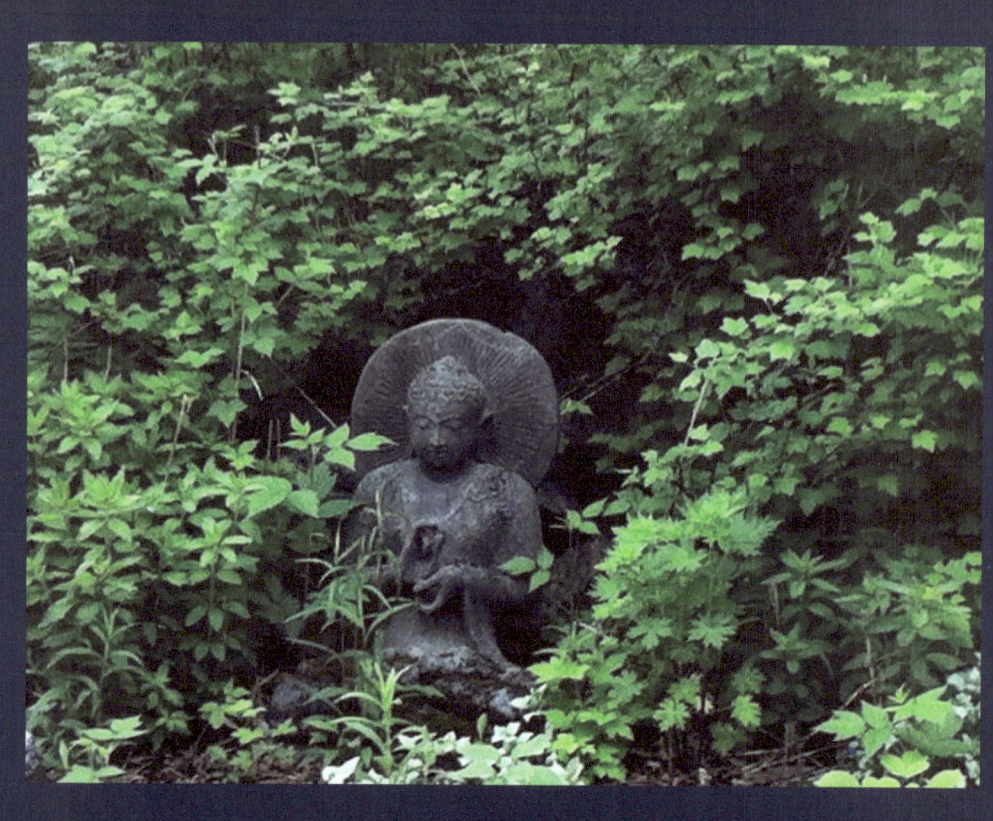